vines

second edition

buyer's guide to canadian wine

vines

second edition

by Walter Sendzik and Christopher Waters

foreword by Steven Page

whitecap

Visit our web site at www.whitecap.ca

Edited by Marial Shea
Proofread by Ann-Marie Metten
Cover concept by Maxine Lea
Cover layout and art direction by Roberta Batchelor
Interior design by Margaret Lee / bamboosilk.com
Cover photograph by Corbis®

Printed and bound in Canada

National Library of Canada Cataloguing in Publication Data
Sendzik, Walter
    Vines buyer's guide to Canadian wines/Walter Sendzik
    and Christopher Waters.

    Includes index.
    ISBN 1-55285-410-8

    1. Wine and wine making—Canada. 2. Wine and wine making —Canada—
Handbooks, manuals etc. I. Waters, Christoper. II. Title. III. Title: Buyer's guide to
Canadian wine.
TP559.C3S45 2002   641.2'2'0971   C2002-911065-3

The publisher acknowledges the support of the Canada Council for the Arts
and the Cultural Services Branch of the Government of British Columbia for our
publishing program. We acknowledge the financial support of the Government
of Canada through the Book Publishing Industry Development Program for our
publishing activities.

> For a free copy of *Vines* magazine,
> contact us at 1-888-883-3372.

CONTENTS

FOREWORD

In rock and roll, we have what is infamously known as the Rider, an addition to the concert contract which states, among other things, what is to be provided in the artist's dressing room. Van Halen insisted on M&Ms with the brown ones removed. Paul McCartney demands that no meat or meat products be present anywhere in the building. Next tour, mine will just say "Read this" with a copy of the *Vines Buyer's Guide to Canadian Wine.* All the promoter will have to do is flip open a couple of pages, send someone down to the local liquor store and my dressing room will be fit for a king or, say, a rock star.

Some really great wines are made in Canada these days, and I've been fortunate enough to be able to taste many of them, some for sheer pleasure and some in academic scrutiny in the preparation of this guide. My wife and I hosted some of the tastings at our home in Toronto. In tasting flights of between thirty and one hundred different wines of each varietal, from vintages ranging from 1998 to 2001, we learned so much about the various styles of winemaking now in practice across the country. From hand-crafted boutique wines, much like the vaunted cult wines of California or Bordeaux's *garagistes,* to mass-produced wines for all price levels, to industrial dreck, Canada's wine industry is profiling the rest of the world quite faithfully.

At the same time, we are making wines that reflect our unique climate, and each regional microclimate, or *terroir,* if I may. With the modern trend towards buying local produce, it seems only natural to match it with local wines. We all know that a locally grown tomato, picked at the right time, will simply blow away any of the hothouse models that we see in shops the rest of the year. While local wine may not be as long-lived or even as respected as its Old World cousin, it's ours, and it's delicious. So whether our shopping choices are political or patriotic, aesthetic or budgetary, there is something in Canadian wine for everyone.

In Canada, most industries have to battle public perception every step of the way. I too carry with me memories of boxes of some of the worst wine imaginable, usable only for attracting fruit flies in my kitchen. I also have more recent recollections of pretentiously packaged bottles of plonk at extreme prices, wines that dare to charge the same as a reputable, reliable and high-quality brand from California, France or Germany. While one is a rip-off and the other a turn-off, I think that neither of these crimes should be blamed on their Canadian-ness. Countless times I've been told that my band was "pretty good for a Canadian band," and let me tell you that it's one of the most offensive passive-aggressive insults I've ever been handed.

I'd like to be good on my own terms, and I think that Canada's wine industry is grown-up enough to be judged the same way. With Canadian wine making up approximately thirty per cent of Canada's overall wine purchases, there's a lot of this stuff for the drinking. And it's not all cheap anymore, either.

Here's where *Vines Buyer's Guide* comes in. *Vines* has tasted all of this wine for you (I know, it's a thankless job, but someone has to do it), and we've whittled it down to the Good Stuff. So, armed with this year's buyer's guide, I encourage you to march into your local wine shop, or take a trip to a winery or two, sample the wares and share them with your friends and families. Heck, maybe you could even start an informal wine tasting salon of your own, where you can swirl, smell and taste with others just as curious as yourself. This is what we've tried to do at my house when we've hosted the *Vines* tastings: serious about the wine and the job at hand, but open to new experiences, and ultimately, pleasures. We bring our palates; Walter, Christopher and *Vines* bring their knowledge and expertise. This is for people who don't want to spit. *L'Chaim!*

Steven Page,
Barenaked Ladies,
Toronto

ACKNOWLEDGMENTS

First, thanks go to the entire panel who graciously donated their time to taste a lot of wine. To Anna Ananicz, Marcus Ansems, Peter Bailey, Derek Barnett, Linda Bramble, Laurie Clark, Ray Cornell, Roberto DiDomenico, Steven Duffy, Fred Gamula, Sigrid S. Gertsen-Briand, Jeff Innes, Tim Kerr, Steven Page, Angelo Pavan, Gary Pieterse, Rod Phillips, Gary Pickering, Klaus Reif, Carolyn Ricketts, Karen Rossi, Brian Schmidt, Tom Seaver, Steven Sokolowski, Matthew Speck, Sue-Ann Staff, Ilia Suter, Anna Weiss, Joe Will and Roger Stefan Wills for all of the comments, notes and general discussions about the wine. Without your valuable input, this book would be a shell of what it is.

To Steven Page for writing the foreword to this book. Thank you for sharing your time and talent to help the magazine evolve and develop—and for being such a gracious and generous host for our Toronto tastings. I think it's our turn to entertain you and Carolyn in Niagara.

To Bremner Biscuit Company from Denver, Colorado, the official cracker of the *Vines* tasting panel, for continued support of our efforts. Our purple-tongued tasters salute you!

To Vintage Niagara Adventures and Tammy Kruk for providing bottle wraps for all the tastings. VNA ensured all tastings were indeed blind with their easy-to-use adhesive wrappers. Visit www.vna.on.ca for more information on their range of quality wine accessories.

Further thanks to the awesome team at Whitecap Books for their unwavering commitment to ensuring our second edition made it to print—and into your hands. To Robert

McCullough for believing in Canadian wines enough to publish the second edition.

To all those who have supported the idea that a book like this could be published annually—to Kara Wille, Pat Waters, Melanie Sendzik, Mom and Dad Sendzik and the rest of the Sendzik and Waters clan, we extend a big hug and thanks for putting up with all those weekends spent tasting wine and those endlessly long nights writing this book. (An extra special thanks to Melanie for putting up with the untold number of bottles that clutter the kitchen, basement, hallway and living room of 159 York Street.)

Also to Ali and Scully, who missed out on numerous walks and visits to the park. You now have your masters' undivided attention. Look out squirrels, here we come.

Finally, and most importantly, we would like to acknowledge those in the Canadian wine industry who have supported *Vines Magazine* since our earliest days. *Vines* is an offshoot of your years of hard work. If it were not for the great number of hardworking winemakers and entrepreneurs who have taken the Canadian wine industry to new heights, this book could not have been completed. This buyer's guide is testimony to your tireless efforts to make great wine.

By purchasing this book, you show your support of products that are 100 per cent Canadian. Consider buying another copy; it would make a great stocking stuffer or birthday gift for the wine enthusiasts on your list.

INTRODUCTION

A funny thing happens when you taste through 1,000 or more wines: an unerring picture of quality comes into focus. In the weeks and months of panel tastings for the second edition of this buyer's guide, we tasted every major and emerging varietal and style produced in Ontario and British Columbia for a snapshot of how the homegrown character of each is developing.

Canadian wine has never been better. And it's getting better all the time.

Wine tells us something new with every vintage. The life-enhancing drink is a reflection of its growing region's unique climate, soil, location and weather conditions, which all impact on the flavours and quality of the finished product.

Canadian wine tells how imagination and commitment have laid the groundwork for wine regions every bit as good as any the rest of the world has to offer. Ontario and British Columbia at their best rival Napa, Burgundy or Bordeaux.

Looking back, we note that it has been only in the past twenty-five years that winemakers began to focus on producing quality, European-styled, vinifera wines. Sure, back in the 1960s and 1970s, Canadian wineries produced blended table wine and a lot of "pop" wines, which sold very well, but a shift took place in the Canadian wine industry in the mid 1970s that revolutionized the quality of the wines.

Led by mavericks such as Karl Kaiser and Donald Ziraldo (who opened Inniskillin, Canada's first estate winery in 1975), Paul Bosc Sr. of Château des Charmes and Joe Pohorly, founder of Newark Winery (which would become Hillebrand Estates Winery after he sold it), the industry started to focus on producing varietal wines from French hybrid and European vinifera grapes. In British Columbia, the pioneering spirit was furthered by Harry McWatters of Sumac Ridge Estate Winery, George Heiss of Gray Monk Cellars and Bob and Lee Claremont, who opened the first estate winery in British Columbia—the now-defunct Claremont—in 1979.

These visionaries had the nerve and the commitment to challenge the status quo. Although many doubted their collective belief that classic vinifera vines such as Chardonnay, Riesling, Cabernet Franc and Merlot could be successfully planted in certain areas of Canada, these pioneers went out and proved that Canada could sustain and produce quality grapes, especially in Niagara and the Okanagan Valley. These were planted along with French hybrids such as Vidal, Baco Noir and Maréchal Foch, and by the early 1980s, a small number of wineries were crafting surprisingly well-made wines.

After it was demonstrated that the fertile soils and climate conditions of southern Ontario and the Okanagan Valley could yield consistent vinifera wines, a second wave of winemakers emerged in the 1980s. Producers such as Colio Wines, Cave Spring Cellars, Pelee Island Winery, Reif Estate Winery and Vineland Estates in Ontario and Calona Wines, Gehringer Brothers and Quails' Gate in British Columbia gave the fledgling industry an extra boost.

These vintners went on to inspire a wave of quality-minded wineries. Some of these include amateur-turned-pro operations Marynissen Estates and Lakeview Cellars in Niagara, as well as farm-gate producers Henry of Pelham Family Estate and Pillitteri Estates in Niagara and Blue Mountain Vineyard and Cellars, St. Hubertus Vineyard and Wild Goose Vineyards in the Okanagan Valley.

Much of the activity in the late 1980s and early 1990s was inspired by NAFTA (the North American Free Trade Agreement), as well as the founding of the Vintners Quality Alliance, first in Ontario in 1989, then in British Columbia in 1990. The spectre of a flood of bulk jug wine from California pouring into Canada led domestic wineries to ratchet up the quality of the wine they were producing so they could establish their own niche at the nation's liquor stores.

Instituting winemaking standards through the VQA, which represents the best Canada has to offer in the way of domestic wine, helped achieve that goal. It was a pivotal move taken by the industry to ensure the quality of the wines being produced. It brought the wineries in British Columbia and Ontario together, working to promote Canadian wines at a time when most people didn't believe in them. Many quality-minded wineries operating outside of the VQA also focus their production on 100 per cent product-of-Canada wines.

The latest surge is a wave of super-premium producers, wineries such as Burrowing Owl Vineyards, CedarCreek Estate Winery and Paradise Ranch Winery in British Columbia and Creekside Estate, Daniel Lenko Estate Winery, The Malivoire Wine Company, Thirty Bench Vineyard and Thirteenth Street Wine Company in Niagara. All are looking to hit a high note with quality vintages made with low yields of carefully farmed fruit.

With Canadian wineries routinely bringing home top awards from international competitions, the quality of domestic wine has never been better. Unfortunately, consumer support for Canadian wine across the country hasn't kept pace. Certainly Icewine is always going to be the specialty item that carries the banner for Canadian wineries into the international arena, but there's more to the industry than sweet dessert wines. Canadian table wines are snapping up medals at VinItaly, the International Wine and Spirit Competition in London, England, and other prestigious world-class wine events. Our reds are beginning to stand shoulder-to-shoulder with well-known reds from California, Australia and Europe. And yet, consumers are still reluctant to buy Canadian wines.

That's where this book can help. We designed this second edition to make it easier for consumers to find, learn about and buy Canadian wines. We've arranged the wines by grape variety or style. If you're a fan of Chardonnay, for example, the Chardonnay section will give you general information about the varietal and how it's produced in Canada. We follow this with an exhaustive review section on Chardonnays made by Canadian wineries, starting with the best in the nation and ranking the wines from "Highly Recommended" to "Recommended" to "Quite Good." The same format applies to all widely planted grape varieties. In the case of lesser-known varieties, they have been grouped together for your convenience.

After tasting the broad range of wines produced in Ontario and British Columbia, we were reminded of the wonderful experience—the wide range of tastes and flavours—that only wine can bring to the senses. There's nothing faddish about great wine. It stimulates passions and emotions. It makes memories. It evokes a certain wow factor.

Many have said that Canadian wines are one of our best-kept secrets, but we feel it's time to spread the word. Wine is best enjoyed with family and friends. By highlighting these exciting bottles, we welcome you to join in the celebration.

About *Vines* Magazine

Vines magazine grew out of our conviction that there was an audience for a magazine that explored and celebrated the good life of wine. Our belief is that the appreciation of wine is part of a multidimensional lifestyle. People who drink wine also lead active lives and have a wide variety of other interests, so why should we place wine in a vacuum, isolated from everything else that stimulates and enriches our lives?

We wanted to put something on the newsstands that makes it clear to you that we understand and respect your approach to wine, your knowledge of it and your broad range of experiences with it.

For the past five years we have been providing readers with a magazine that transcends the staid, pretentious view of wine upheld by other wine publications. We were the first wine magazine in Canada to view wine as part of a lifestyle, not as a hobby or an elite club. Readers have come to understand that, with *Vines*, their interest in wine is encouraged to develop through personal experimentation. They are appreciated for their level of wine knowledge, not lectured on it. It's a small, but very significant point.

We believed that casual consumers who enjoy a glass of wine would pick up a wine magazine without feeling intimidated if the publication spoke to them. It was an idea that wine writing can be both entertaining and educational. By placing wine in a cultural context, which includes music, food, art, literature and so much more, we have given readers a larger forum from which they can build their own personal experiences with wine.

And the key element in this tale of a dream reaching fruition is the people behind the conviction. We're not wine snobs—you can trust me on that one. We love wine for what it is: a work of art that conveys stories on so many different levels. For more information on *Vines Magazine*, visit our web site at www.vinesmag.com.

How Were the Reviews Created?

A collective of people created the reviews for the buyer's guide. The process started back in February 2002 when a fax was sent to all the wineries in British Columbia and Ontario. The request was for wineries to submit wines available to the consumer through 2002–03—whether at liquor stores or through wine shops and boutiques. The stipulation was that the wine must be VQA certified and/or use 100 per cent grown-in-Canada grapes. Within weeks, the *Vines* office was flooded with cases of wine. The boxes took over an entire floor of our St. Catharines operation. Once all the wines were entered into our database—more than 1,000 were submitted this year—we divided up the varieties and began the long process of organizing the panel tastings. Recognizing that everyone has a different palate, we wanted to have diverse panels with different members to fully explore the wines each time. Panels consisted of three to five people. Walter Sendzik and Christopher Waters were the regulars, with winemakers, wine educators, sommeliers, wine enthusiasts and wine consumers rounding out the panel.

Within their respective groups, we divided the wines by vintage and then by reserve and and other meaningful classifications. All tastings were done blind, which means that the panel members only knew the wine type, but not the producer or the region where it was produced. This allowed for the greatest amount of objectivity. Each panel member was directed to score the wines based on the *Vines Magazine* five-star rating system. They were also asked to give detailed descriptions of the wine. At the end of each tasting, we collected the tasting sheets and compiled the scores and accorded each wine its ranking.

The difference between reviews in this buyer's guide and others written by wine critics is that these are much more accurate, being based on a collective resource of information versus the opinions and peccadilloes of just one person.

And finally, Walter Sendzik and Christopher Waters wrote all the reviews. We approached each review with the consumer in mind. Our goal was to educate and entertain. The reviews are a reflection of the wine—the higher the ranking, the more verbose the review. And wines are also a part of our culture—we know you'll be able to relate to our cultural references.

Who Are the Reviewers?

Anna Ananicz, sommelier, St. Catharines

Marcus Ansems, winemaker, Creekside Estate Winery, Jordan Station

Peter Bailey, editorial page editor, *St. Catharines Standard*, St. Catharines

Derek Barnett, winemaker, Lailey Vineyards, Niagara-on-the-Lake

Dr. Linda Bramble, sommelier, wine writer, educator and industry liaison for the Cool Climate Oenology and Viticulture Institute, Brock University, St. Catharines

Laurie Clark, wine enthusiast, Toronto

Ray Cornell, winemaker, Harvest Estates Wines and Hernder Estates Winery, St. Catharines

Roberto DiDomenico, winemaker, Reif Estate Winery, Niagara-on-the-Lake

Steven Duffy, musician and wine lover, London, UK

Fred Gamula, chief sommelier of Vintage Inns, Niagara-on-the-Lake

Sigrid S. Gertsen-Briand, Lallemand Specialty Fermentation Products, Niagara-on-the-Lake

Jeff Innes, winemaker, Three Sisters Winery, Georgia, USA

Tim Kerr, freelance wine writer, Grimsby

Steven Page, Barenaked Ladies lead singer and wine lover, Toronto

Angelo Pavan, winemaker, Cave Spring Cellars, Jordan

Gary Pieterse, consumer, Fonthill

Dr. Rod Phillips, *Ottawa Citizen* wine writer, senior editor *Vines* magazine, sommelier, director of the National Capital Sommelier Guild and author of *A Short History of Wine* (Penguin UK, 2000), Ottawa

Dr. Gary Pickering, oenologist and sensory scientist, Cool Climate Oenology and Viticulture Institute, Brock University, St. Catharines

Klaus Reif, winemaker and president, Reif Estate Winery, Niagara-on-the-Lake

Carolyn Ricketts, wine enthusiast, Toronto

Karen Rossi, sommelier, Pillar and Post, Niagara-on-the-Lake

Brian Schmidt, winemaker, Vineland Estates Winery, Vineland

Tom Seaver, winemaker, Jackson-Triggs Niagara Estate
Winery, Niagara-on-the-Lake

Walter Sendzik, publisher/editor of *Vines* magazine, co-author of the *Vines Buyer's Guide to Canadian Wine*, St. Catharines

Steven Sokolowski, wine collector, Toronto

Matthew Speck, vice president/viticulturalist, Henry of Pelham Family Estate Winery, St. Catharines

Sue-Ann Staff, winemaker, Pillitteri Estates Winery, Niagara-on-the-Lake

Ilia Suter, assistant winemaker, Cave Spring Cellars, Jordan

Christopher Waters, managing editor of *Vines* magazine, co-author of the *Vines Buyer's Guide to Canadian Wine*, wine columnist for the *St. Catharines Standard*

Anna Weiss, grape grower, St. Catharines

Joe Will, winemaker and owner, Strewn Wines Inc., Niagara-on-the-Lake

Roger Stefan Wills, chef and patron, Café Brussel, Toronto

The *Vines* Magazine Rating System

Our rating is based on a five-star system. A score is given only after a thorough, objective assessment of the wine's qualities. After each panelist submits a rating for the wine, the ratings are aggregated and the wine is awarded a ranking within the five-star system.

Vines Award *****

To achieve this ranking the wine must be of outstanding quality. The panel awards this mark if the wine is the best of the tasting. In some cases, the panel has decided that the top wines did not reach the level of superlative quality and therefore some sections in the book will not have a *Vines* Award.

Highly Recommended ****

For a wine to achieve this ranking it must be a truly exceptional example of its grape variety.

Recommended ***

These are wines that have positive characteristics that were singled out by our panel.

Quite Good **

All are good, quaffable wines.

Acceptable *

Decent wine, free of faults. This category of faint-praise reviews, used in *Vines* magazine, is omitted in this book to save space for showcasing only the finest wines produced in Canada.

Note: Wines that were deemed faulted or not suitable for recommendation in a buyer's guide were not reviewed.

How to Read the Reviews

This is the ranking category

Winery

Vintage and proper
name of wine

Appellation recognized
by the VQA

VINES AWARD

Mission Hill Family Estate Winery
1999 Merlot Reserve
Okanagan Valley VQA $$ (496109)
When the panel tasted Mission Hill's 1999 Merlot,
it was hard for them to believe it indeed came
from a Canadian producer. Lush notes of blue-
berry and vanilla filled the glass. Wonderful
flavours of blueberry, blackcurrant and hints of
pine and cedar illustrate its complexity. Warm,
soft and supple, this Merlot has it all.

Vintners Quality Alliance

Price of wine by
category based, on
province of origin:
$ less than $15
$$ $16 to $25
$$$ $26 to $35
$$$$ more than $35

CSPU number (If a
wine does not have a
number, it means it is
sold only at the winery)

CANADIAN WINE REGIONS

British Columbia

British Columbia has four designated grape growing
regions that are recognized as viticultural areas by VQA
Canada. The largest of the four is the **Okanagan Valley**,
in the central southern part of British Columbia, nestled
in the Cascade Mountain Range that runs through into
Washington State. Nearby is a much smaller viticultural
area, the **Similkameen Valley**. The other two viticultural
areas are the **Fraser Valley** and **Vancouver Island**, which
are both considered coastal regions.

According to the British Columbia Wine Institute, the
province has approximately 5,000 acres of vineyards dedicated to wine production. There are over seventy wineries
in British Columbia, although most are farmgate companies
that produce only small amounts of wine.

Similar to Ontario's history of wine production, British
Columbia's started back in the 1930s with plantings of
Labrusca varieties such as Concord, Niagara, Patricia,
Sheridan and Bath. Although the Okanagan Valley was a
natural site for vineyard development since apple orchards
flourished in the area, it was Growers' Wine Company and
Victoria Wineries located on Vancouver Island that, as early
as 1930, first produced wines from the local Labrusca
grapes. The Okanagan's oldest winery, Calona Wines, was
established in 1936.

Concentrated vineyard development took hold in the
1960s when the B.C. government encouraged the planting
of vines by passing a law that stated wines made in the
province had to contain a minimum of twenty-five per cent

B.C. grown grapes. Andrew Peller, a pioneer in the Canadian wine industry, built Andrés Wines in 1961 in Port Moody. Other wineries opened and closed, among them the first incarnation of Mission Hill Winery.

Just as the first car ever built wasn't a Cadillac or Corvette, the wines produced during the early years of B.C.'s modern wine history were not palate pleasers. Created from French and American hybrids such as De Chaunac, Maréchal Foch, Verdelet, Baco Noir and Okanagan Riesling, the wines were palatable, but not exactly noble in comparison to classic vinifera wines from the Old World. But the mini-boom, started with the support of the B.C. government and entrepreneurial minds of people such as Peller, led farmers to turn orchards into vineyards, creating an environment that would eventually lead to experimentations with vinifera varieties.

By the late 1970s, the B.C. government once again stepped in to help the wine industry. Wineries were permitted to open on-site retail stores and grants were provided to allow farmers to experiment with other grape varietals such as Pinot Blanc, Gewürztraminer and Ehrenfelser. As well, legislation was introduced that created estate wineries by stipulating that estate or cottage wineries had to have twenty acres of vineyard, could only produce up to 30,000 gallons of wine and had to use 100 per cent grapes from British Columbia, of which fifty per cent had to come from the estate. The first estate winery to open under the new act was Claremont in 1979.

The 1980s saw an influx of small estate wineries that took advantage of the provincial government's support of the wine industry. Early farmgate winery pioneers such as Sumac Ridge and Gray Monk and entrepreneurs such as Anthony von Mandl, who purchased a dilapidated winery in 1981 once known as—and eventually renamed—Mission Hill, led the charge to build a modern wine industry in British Columbia.

As in Ontario, the North American Free Trade Agreement in 1988 had an enormous impact on the grape growing industry in British Columbia. Growers were paid by the federal government to rip out Labrusca and French hybrid grapes and plant vinifera whites such as Riesling, Gewürztraminer, Chardonnay, Pinot Blanc, Pinot Gris and red vinifera such as Pinot Noir, Merlot and Cabernet Sauvignon. The program was aimed at increasing the quality of grapes to help offset the flood of bulk wine that was feared would pour into Canada once the trade barriers were removed with NAFTA. Although resisted in the beginning by growers, NAFTA proved to be a key in getting the Canadian wine industry to the next level.

Since the early 1990s, with the year-over-year increase in vinifera wines from British Columbia, the industry has taken off. With a lot of support from B.C. consumers and restaurants, which is not the case in Ontario, wineries in British Columbia have established a strong presence in the Pacific Northwest. Wineries such as Calona Wines with talented winemaker Howard Soon, Mission Hill Family Estate Winery with its New Zealand-born winemaker John Simes and Jackson-Triggs Okanagan Estate Winery's Aussie winemaker Bruce Nichol, are all creating wines that have taken home major international awards. And medium-sized wineries such as Quails' Gate Estate Winery and Tinhorn Creek Estate Winery have become stalwarts in creating consistently high-end, quality wines. With the supporting cast of farmgate wineries such as Hester Creek Winery, Hillside Estates, Lake Breeze Winery and La Frenz Winery, which are intent on making small-batch, premium wines, the reputation of British Columbia wineries as producers of excellent wine is quickly growing on the international stage.

The biggest question that needs to be answered, both in British Columbia and Ontario, is which grape produces most consistently in making great wines? Considering that ninety-five per cent of the grape production in British Columbia comes from the Okanagan Valley, it's the best place to look at how well certain grapes perform. Since 1998, when we started producing guides to Canadian wines, we have noted the best-performing wines each year. Based on the results of our tastings and interviews with winemakers, it's clear that the northern part of the Okanagan

Valley, from Summerland and up, is better suited for whites such as Chardonnay, Gewürztraminer, Sauvignon Blanc, Pinot Blanc and Pinot Gris. The growing season can be as much as two to three weeks earlier between this area and the southern part of the valley. Although arid by nature, the entire valley uses irrigation in creating ideal conditions for the grapes.

The southern part of the Okanagan Valley, from Oliver to Osoyoos, bordering Washington State, is home to Canada's only desert, and the conditions are hot. A longer growing season in this area produces highly concentrated reds such as Merlot, Cabernet Sauvignon and Pinot Noir. Over the past few years, wineries have scooped up most of the remaining land in the south and it's now a hot spot for vineyard development. Wine giants such as Jackson-Triggs and Mission Hill have invested heavily in the area. With controlled irrigation and aging vines, the level of quality red wines being pro-duced has taken off. Merlot is definitely a wine to watch from British Columbia, as is Cabernet Sauvignon.

And don't forget Icewine. Although not as well known around the world as Ontario is for its Icewine, British Columbia's Okanagan Valley has the potential every year to produce it. An arctic blast in December or January usually allows for the perfect conditions. Pinot Blanc, Ehrenfelser and Chardonnay Icewine are starting to establish a niche market, and even Pinot Noir Icewine was made in 2000 by Calona Wines.

The future looks bright for British Columbia's wine industry. With continued investment from the industry, a constant drive from the winemakers to produce better wines every year and continued support from con-sumers, B.C. wines will be a player on the international wine scene in the next few years.

Okanagan Valley

The Okanagan Valley, nestled in the Cascade Mountains, produces close to ninety-five per cent of British Columbia wines. Historically, the Okanagan Valley has been known as a fruit orchard belt, with apples, cherries and peaches as the staple products. Over the past two decades, grape growers and wineries have established grapes as a leading product of the area. Home to seventy wineries and 222 grape growers, it has 5,000 acres under vines. Dry, hot summer conditions are tempered by irrigation from the immense Okanagan Lake.

Similkameen Valley

An offshoot of the Okanagan, located over a mountain range west of the southern Okanagan Valley, the Similkameen Valley is home to a handful of wineries. Desert-like conditions are relieved by irrigation from the Similkameen River. This area has yet to establish itself as a major player.

Fraser Valley

The grape-growing region closest to Greater Vancouver, the Fraser Valley has been growing grapes since the 1960s. It is not overly populated with wineries, with only three in the area, but it is home to Andrés Wines in Port Moody.

Vancouver Island

The most westerly-designated grape growing region in Canada, Vancouver Island has revived its winemaking past. With fourteen wineries situated on the Island, it appears there's enough confidence to make wine in this more humid and wet growing season. All the wineries are small estate companies that barely produce enough to satisfy more than the local restaurants. The results are varied and the jury is still out as to how well these wineries can make the wine and if they will ever be more than just small players in the industry.

For more information on British Columbia's wine industry check out www.winebc.com.

Ontario

Before the War of 1812, a retired German solider grew Labrusca grapes and made wine from them on a plot of land near Mississauga. Though more than fifty years would pass before a commercial operation would hang out its shingle, Corporal Johann Schiller stands as Ontario's winemaking pioneer.

The first commercial winery in Canada was established in 1866 on Pelee Island, located in Lake Erie. The remains of the building, Vin Villa, still stand today, not far from the flourishing Pelee Island Winery. Pelee Island Winery has a string of retail shops, is the best-selling Vintners Quality Alliance producer in the Liquor Control Board of Ontario and has an expansive web site that accepts online orders. One wonders exactly how expansive a market Vin Villa had in its day.

Winery development flourished from the late 1800s to the early 1900s, with as many as forty wineries in operation across the province. The industry continued to develop even through Prohibition (1916 to 1927), when the Canadian Temperance Act allowed for wine to be the only alcohol sold legally. In addition to local sales, an active bootleg trade between the border cities meant Ontario wineries enjoyed strong, if illegal, sales to our American cousins.

Adhemar de Chaunac, who planted forty different European grape varieties in Niagara Peninsula, including Chardonnay and Pinot Noir, conducted the first experimentation with grapes other than the native Labrusca varieties in 1946. The results were mixed, to say the least. As late as the 1970s, growers who invested in vineyards planted to Chardonnay, Riesling, Pinot Noir and others of the so-called "noble" vinifera grape varieties were considered by some to be foolhardy. We know better today. In fact, now many of those early vineyards are the source for the Old Vines Chardonnay and Old Vines Merlot bottlings that are featured in the reserve portfolios of some wineries.

The chief output of Ontario's wineries was a wide variety of blended wines, often labelled as "ports" and "sherries." They were high in sugar and alcohol content—"there was a fight in every bottle," recalls my grandfather. Lower alcohol, drier wines began to gain popularity in the 1960s and 1970s.

The spark of transformation occurred in 1975 when Inniskillin was granted the first estate winery licence in Ontario since Prohibition. A number of estate wineries followed in its wake, including Pelee Island Winery and Colio Estates Wines, located in what would be designated the Lake Erie North Shore viticultural area.

The inception of the Free Trade Agreement with the United States in 1988 resulted in a rapid transformation of the province's vineyards, as two-thirds of the acreage planted with Labrusca grapes were ripped out and replanted with vinifera and French hybrid grape varieties. Even then, suspicion of the long-term viability of vinifera grapes, including Chardonnay, Pinot Noir, Merlot and Gewürztraminer, led to widescale planting of Vidal, Seyval Blanc, Maréchal Foch and Baco Noir.

A year later, the Vintners Quality Alliance was created with eighteen founding members. The alliance created a province-wide appellation system that detailed production and quality standards and regulations for winemaking. The system designated three viticultural areas: Lake Erie North Shore, Pelee Island and Niagara Peninsula, the area surrounding the southern tip of Lake Ontario, which accounts for eighty per cent of the country's growing volume.

A decade later, when the VQA Act was proclaimed into law in Ontario, there were fifty-two VQA producing wineries. The act cemented the quality regulations and, best of all for consumers, created an enforcement arm that oversees comprehensive audits and periodic reviews of products available at winery retail stores, LCBO outlets and at licensees. Producers are accountable for producing wines that live up to VQA standards.

The growth of wineries continues at a rapid rate. More than ninety winery licences are issued in Ontario, including cottage fruit wineries. Meanwhile acreage for wine grapes in Ontario amounts to more than 17,000 acres. Chardonnay remains the most popular single varietal, followed by Riesling and Cabernet Franc.

The VQA is currently studying the potential of naming sub-appellations within the existing three designated viticultural areas, looking at growing regions that reflect unique characteristics of their area, with likely candidates being the Beamsville Bench and the Niagara-on-the-Lake plains.

If this talk of behind-the-scenes administration of the VQA leaves you cold (and you'd be forgiven for stifling a yawn at the mention of sub-appellations and other industry machinations), steel your determination with the fact that the VQA represents the future of the Canadian wine industry. Created in Ontario and adopted in British Columbia, it has established the framework for the growth and development of quality winemaking.

And the future looks bright, both at home and on the international front. Niagara's industry has benefitted from recently announced Franco-Canadian joint-ventures, including Le Clos Jordan, an impressive start-up created by the country's largest wine company, Vincor International, and the Boisset Family of Burgundy. Le Clos Jordan is dedicated to creating world-class Pinot Noir and Chardonnay. Canadian-born architectural visionary Frank Gehry has been commissioned to build the winery, which will focus even greater international attention on Ontario and its winemaking capabilities.

As we stated in the introduction, Canadian wine has never been better. And, it's getting better all the time. But to truly understand the Canadian wine industry, you have to taste the wines. There's plenty to try. Read on and we'll help you narrow your focus somewhat.

For more information about Ontario wines check out www.wineroute.com.

WHITE WINE

CHARDONNAY

In the world of wine, Chardonnay remains king. Although waning, its popularity is still such that most wine drinkers think white wine is synonymous with Chardonnay. What's puzzling about its great appeal, however, is that few consumers know Chardonnay's actual flavour because the wine is made in such a wide range of styles. Perhaps the root of its allure is its French-bred sophistication, or perhaps it is simply that mass-produced Chardonnay is a smooth, generally straightforward, easy-drinking wine.

Chardonnay has taken its share of knocks, particularly from the ABC (Anything But Chardonnay) contingent of consumers who decried it as being about as appetizing as getting thwacked in the head with a two-by-four. The description is an apt one. New World Chardonnay producers went a little overboard with oak aging

FOOD PAIRING SUGGESTIONS
What goes with Chardonnay? What doesn't is more the question. Considering the range of styles, there's an equally broad range of potential matches for the wines. Lighter wines are generally more food friendly, while some of the heavier oaked wines require more robust meals. Try dry and delicate *sur lie* wines with oysters and shellfish. Bigger wines can muscle in on salmon, roast chicken and veal with cream sauce or earthy mushrooms.

and other winemaking techniques in a go-big-or-go-home bout of one-upsmanship. Both the true varietal character of Chardonnay and its traditional consumer got left behind as vintners produced titanic wines, whoppers with fourteen-plus per cent alcohol that were too big for the wine glass and too surly for the dinner table.

We're happy to announce that those days are over and boldly predict that Chardonnay's renaissance has arrived. The *Vines* panel spent four days tasting through the eighteen cases of Chardonnay submitted and were uniformly impressed by the across-the-board quality of the wines. The days of over-oaked, over-amped Chardonnay are behind us, as winemakers have learned to listen to the vineyard and let the fruit speak to them.

The easy-to-produce, easy-to-enjoy white is a delight for all parties concerned—grape grower, winemaker and consumer. The vines flourish in early spring, giving the early ripening variety a head start throughout the growing season.

Once in the winery, Chardonnay is fashioned in a wide range of styles by aging it in oak, on its lees (dead yeast cells spent during fermentation) or entirely in stainless steel to preserve and focus its fruit flavours. The process greatly affects the flavour, texture and weight of the finished wine. Not all Chardonnays, then, are created equal, which makes it all the more crucial to understand labelling terminology.

Joe Will, owner and winemaker of Strewn Wines in Niagara-on-the-Lake, said his goal is to create Chardonnay that reflects its vineyard site. Reducing the crop and removing leaves to maximize sun exposure are two techniques he uses to ensure his fruit ripens to maturity. "Our goal is to get it nicely ripe, let it get a little higher in alcohol, which adds the flavour development," he said, explaining that his focus on fruit continues in the winery. "We use only brand new barrels. Although we do oak, it's only a touch for complexity. We don't want to overwhelm what the grape brings to the story."

The work in the vineyard is crucial for crafting great Chardonnay, agreed Tom DiBello, winemaker for Okanagan Valley winery CedarCreek, who scored a *Vines* Award for his 2000 Estate Chardonnay. "I have worked all over the world," says DiBello, "and I will say the Chardonnay here is as good or better than any I've seen over the past twenty years as long as your viticulture is top-notch."

If you're a fan of crisp, fruity Chardonnays, you're looking to land an unoaked model. The lack of consensus on labelling, however, means you'll be staring down everything from non-oaked, unoaked or no oak designations. Surely, oak free isn't far off.

Also on the lighter side, *sur lie* Chardonnays are improved with a lush, creamy texture from the winemaking technique of aging the wine on top of its lees. The dead yeast cells impart a pleasant yeasty, nutty flavour to the wine.

Chardonnays that have seen some oak are generally easier to spot: "barrel aged" or "barrel fermented" will be featured prominently on the label, partially to justify the sticker price. Oak aging, particularly when done in French *barriques* adds to the expense of the finished wine. Oak aging mellows the acidity and fruit, but if not properly handled, it can overwhelm the positive characteristics and make for a clumsy wine. Think of it like adding spice in cooking. A little taste can perk up a dish, adding depth of flavour and some interest to your meal. Too much spoils the meal.

The real can of worms in terms of Chardonnay labels is reserve bottles, which are often—but not always—more focussed and refined than their barrel-aged brethren. As with other domestic wines, the term "reserve" is not defined by law. Essentially, it means whatever the winery wants it to mean. Consumers assume that "reserve" connotes the vintner's best selection, but that's not written in stone.

Tasting Panel: AA, LB, RP, TS, WS, SAS, CW

VINES AWARD

Cave Spring Cellars 1999 CSV Chardonnay
Niagara Peninsula $$$ (529941)

Cave Spring's CSV reserve is a taut, refreshing, food-friendly, age-worthy Chardonnay that tastes something like a blend between an elegant Puligny Montrachet and smouldering Mersault. It matters not if those Burgundy touchstones mean anything to you. What's important for you to know is that this is a seriously great Chardonnay with grip and finesse. Impressive richness with forceful fruit, mineral notes and classy oak framing combine to create an extraordinary wine you won't forget.

CedarCreek Estate Winery 2000 Chardonnay Estate Select
Okanagan Valley $$ (607200)

The best B.C. bottle in our tasting, this Chardonnay drew raves from panelists with its ripe, attractive fruit flavours, creamy texture and fine balance. The fruit gains complexity from a rich hickory smoke note. This fabulously flavourful wine will take your guests from sitting room or deck to the dinner table without missing a beat. Enjoy with seafood, chicken or pasta served with cream sauce or fruit chutneys. Heaven.

Inniskillin Wines 2000 Chardonnay
Seeger Vineyard

Niagara Peninsula $$ (586362)

This is simply an extraordinary Chardonnay at its price. A full-bodied dry white wine from Albrecht Seeger's Niagara-on-the-Lake vineyard, it offers a complex and fascinating flavour profile: herbs, minerals, figs, vanilla, nuts and melons. It deserves to be served with roast poultry or, better yet, salmon.

HIGHLY RECOMMENDED

Cave Spring Cellars 1999 Reserve Chardonnay

Niagara Peninsula $$ (256522)

Cave Spring's reserve is a delightful floral and spice scented white wine for late spring quaffing. It comes right at you with generous fruit, especially peach, pear and apple flavours, and some light cedar and lavender notes. Soft and rich, it boasts amazing concentration and a rich core of spicy fruit flavours. "Excellent" was one taster's curt synopsis. You can serve it by itself, but it will show better if paired with seafood or spicy cuisine.

CedarCreek Estate Winery 2000 Chardonnay
Platinum Reserve

Okanagan Valley $$$ (607218)

New Wave is back in a big way, thanks to dashing bands like the White Stripes and the Hives, who play rock and roll the way Mick and Keef used to. One taste of CedarCreek's equally flashy Chardonnay, and we're ready to start a fan club. It's as stylish and flat-out pleasurable as the Hives's *Your New Favourite Band* CD, with its expressive fruit, bright acidity, deep oak tones and long lingering finish. Ladies and gentlemen, prepare to flick your Bics. Hello, Okanagan Valley … Hello, world.

Creekside Estate Winery 1999 Marcus Ansems Signature Chardonnay

Niagara Peninsula $$$

Creekside's debut Signature reserve vintage offers flavours of lemon, apple, pear, minerals, nuts, spices and even a nuance of coconut. And it presents this mélange of flavours while keeping an exquisite elegance and balance and finishing long and clean. While the wine has plenty of body, it is also elegant. It displays the perfect harmony between power and subtle complexity for which high-end Burgundy Chardonnays are known.

Daniel Lenko Estate Winery 2000 Chardonnay French Oak

Niagara Peninsula $$

Winemakers employ French oak barrels to add some finesse and complexity to their wines. This wine is a textbook example of what *barriques* can do to ripe, concentrated Chardonnay fruit. A gloriously rich, full-bodied wine, it has subtle spice and smoke notes amidst the volleys of ripe fruit that burst over your taste buds.

Henry of Pelham Family Estate Winery 1999 Speck Family Reserve Chardonnay

Niagara Peninsula $$$ (616466)

The top-of-the-line Chardonnay from Henry of Pelham is a suitably impressive combination of power and finesse. Less Shaq and more Kobe Bryant, this showtime wine unleashes lovely rich flavours with added depth from flinty mineral notes and a warm oaky aftertaste. This is a wine of great complexity with good aging potential. Enjoy with smoked trout dishes or roasted red snapper or hake baked over mushroom potatoes.

Hillebrand Estates 2000 Showcase Chardonnay Barrel 9017 (Old American Oak) Huebel Vineyard
Niagara Peninsula $$$ (980995)

This well-made single barrel reserve from Hillebrand Estates has bright pineapple and citrus flavours with complex flint and mineral notes and excellent length. But what makes it truly exceptional is the high level of nervy, racy acidity, making the wine a delicious match for oysters now and promising a wine that will improve in the bottle for a few years.

Southbrook Winery 2000 Chardonnay Triomphe
Niagara Peninsula $$

Call this the wine-world equivalent to action hero Vin Diesel. Intense, rich and bigger than life are all attributes shared by *The Fast and the Furious* star and this blockbuster Chardonnay. Both will muscle their way into your heart. The oak is upfront and beautifully balanced with an equally bold core of fruit. The bright acidity suggests this is a cellar dweller with excellent prospects for a long, fruitful career. Drink now to 2010.

Southbrook Winery 1999 Chardonnay Triomphe
Niagara Peninsula $$ (533315)

The allure of this wine was obvious to all tasters, who were bowled over by its deep citrus and toasted coconut aromas and equally rich and raw palate profile. There's a depth of flavour and concentration to this wine that's impossible to miss. Yet there's also an elegance to the presentation that makes it supremely finer than the blockbuster oak bombs that turned so many consumers off Chardonnay in the past decade. It will be better given two or three years for the component flavours to further integrate and harmonize.

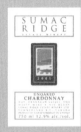

Strewn Wines 1999 Terroir Chardonnay Strewn Vineyard

Niagara Peninsula $$ (542415)

The nose is a mélange of spice, cedar and pear notes that carry over onto the rich and creamy palate. Apple and pear fruit marry assertive oak flavours in this well-integrated and slightly warm Chardonnay. A wine with good weight and complexity. Enjoyable now for its fiery fruit, it will blossom beautifully in the cellar over the next five years.

Sumac Ridge Estate Winery 2001 Chardonnay Unoaked

Okanagan Valley $ (623199)

The charms of this fresh, finely balanced wine are undeniable. Fruit cocktail aromas are followed by rich, ripe fruit flavours, with complex lemon character and ripe tropical fruit on the palate. Full-flavoured enough to enjoy on its own, this wine has enough fat to stand up to the exotic spice of Asian and Thai foods. Vegetarians take note: this wine has a purity of fruit that makes it a fabulous foil for a wide range of salads.

Thirteenth Street Wine Co. 2000 Sandstone Reserve Chardonnay

Niagara Peninsula $$

A solid, fruit-forward style of Chardonnay that's got one foot in Niagara, the other in Burgundy. Buttery toast and vanilla aromas stand out, as do a delicious core of fruit, including loads of apple, peach and pineapple. This is a well-made wine that will make friends easily. It will also undoubtedly become more complex and interesting after its sweet fruit has lost its primary exuberance, so consider it a solid cellar candidate. Don't be ashamed, however, to find you've consumed it all within the year. That fruit is undeniably appealing.

RECOMMENDED

Angels Gate Winery 2000 Old Vines Chardonnay Barrel Aged Beamsville Bench

Niagara Peninsula $$

If children's rhymes are to be believed, girls are made of sugar, spice and everything nice. This vivid wine would have us believe that Chardonnay are similarly crafted with smoke, citrus and a little hit of eucalyptus. The debut vintage from this Beamsville newcomer suggests they'll be one to watch for Chardonnay in the coming years.

Birchwood Estate Wines 2000 Unoaked Chardonnay

Niagara Peninsula $

An extremely aromatic wine, with some Muscat floral notes bobbing around the glass along with tropical and toasted almond aromas. It's soft, rich and complex, with *sur lie* character, and orange citrus flavours that come through nicely on the finish. A delicious everyday, every meal kind of wine—the perfect thing for your favourite armchair activity. A ten-letter word for enjoyment, you ask? Try Chardonnay.

Cave Spring Cellars 2000 Chardonnay

Niagara Peninsula $ (228551)

Here's an easy-drinking style of Chardonnay that puts an emphasis on the ripe fruit character, with a creamy note on the rounded palate, which bursts with mouthwatering acidity. There's a stylish flourish to this wine that belies its lower price tag. An excellent go-to wine. Buy by the case and you've got an all-purpose white to serve by the glass or with mid week bistro fare.

Cave Spring Cellars 2000 Chardonnay Estate
Niagara Peninsula $ (471391)
Made in the Chablis style, this wine offers rich melon notes and an intense, rich structure. Well-balanced, with a long, lingering finish, this is a seriously good wine. Its vibrant flavours will refresh your palate and enhance a wide variety of dining situations—from paper-plate casual to bone-china formal.

Château des Charmes Winery 2000 Chardonnay
Niagara Peninsula $ (056754)
Fresh and pleasing Chardonnay with bright citrus and melon fruit and no discernable oak notes. The fruit is nicely focussed on the palate, which is silky and so very tasty. There are plenty of Chardonnays at twice the price that don't come close to the quality of this wine. Best Buy.

Creekside Estate Winery 2000 Chardonnay
Niagara Peninsula $$ (572198)
Waves of fruit aromas roll out of the glass—citrus, apple, pineapple, melon, passion fruit, peach— and mingle with some nutty almond and hazelnut notes. The fruit gives way on the palate, which boasts a rich creamy texture and peppery intensity from bright acidity and higher alcohol content. This is just the thing to enjoy alongside dishes with rich, creamy sauces.

Daniel Lenko Estate Winery 2000 Chardonnay American Oak
Niagara Peninsula $$
Deep, delicious fruit aromas are moderated on the palate with a slightly astringent finish. This flavourful wine is concentrated and well balanced, but that sharp note spoils the party. Best now with food.

Hawthorne Mountain Vineyards 1999 Mountain Reserve Chardonnay

Okanagan Valley $ (576934)

Packs in a lot of good appley fruit, cedar, spice and some interesting herbal notes, dill and green grass, more common to Sauvignon Blanc than the King of Grapes. The fruit and spice carry over onto the palate, which is crisp and clean, with some creamy character trying to break through. Holds its focus and continues to reveal extra layers of flavour on the lingering finish.

Hillebrand Estates 2000 Showcase Chardonnay Barrel 4089 (New Troncais Oak) Glenlake Vineyard

Niagara Peninsula $$$ (981019)

Another single barrel wine from Hillebrand's expansive Chardonnay collection, this wine offers a mouthful of toffee and restrained-but-ripe fruit that maintains its intensity right through to the finish. It's an easy-drinking, complex style that's appealing. Drink now.

Hillebrand Estates 2000 Showcase Chardonnay Barrel 4094 (New Troncais Oak) Prydatkewycz Vineyard

Niagara Peninsula $$$ (980961)

A nice orchestration of ripe fruit and oak with touches of creamy, toasty oak and rich caramel aromas. Soft and round, this is a different style of Chardonnay, but with sufficient character to make it an interesting wine. Good richness, complexity and depth. Serve as an aperitif or with grilled vegetables, feta and balsamic vinaigrette.

Hillebrand Estates 1999 Showcase Chardonnay Unfiltered (Wine Bottled with Its Lees)

Niagara Peninsula $$$ (981043)

This looks like a snow globe, thanks to the abundant floating yeast cells dancing around in the bottle. Fear not, those solids won't hurt you—hey, it's more protein, it's good for you. They do, however, impart an interesting cedar and matchstick quality to the wine. The flavours run towards spice and some tropical fruit with a flavourful but low intensity finish. A definite novelty wine.

Hillebrand Estates 2000 Trius Chardonnay Beamsville Bench

Niagara Peninsula $$ (291468)

A complex, rich wine, with nice tropical fruit and clove aromas. On the palate the abundant oak spice is nicely matched with the fruit flavours. A slight bitterness on the finish kept this from scoring even higher with panelists.

Hillebrand Estates 2000 Trius Chardonnay Lakeshore

Niagara Peninsula $$ (291484)

A Chardonnay with nice concentration and well-handled oak aging, this benefits from buttery vanilla and spice notes on the palate. A solid choice for roast turkey, salmon on cedar planks or a basket of fresh baked bread and selection of cheese. Try Gruyère, double cream Brie or Camembert.

Inniskillin Okanagan Vineyards 1999 Reserve Chardonnay

Okanagan Valley $ (558411)

Shows off some clove and coriander spice and rich applesauce aromas, and adds some other flavours that are equally spicy and intense. Green pears and spices tickle your tongue and the finish is long and crisp. This wine screams out for butternut squash soup or other rich fall fare.

Inniskillin Wines 2000 Chardonnay Klose Vineyard

Niagara Peninsula $$ (586339)

Although the flavour doesn't scream Chardonnay, this wine's creamy lime notes and restrained oak and *sur lie* character make for an interesting crisp white wine. If you dig oysters, then, by all means, tuck in. This would be a nice partner to Thai-style salads and seafood dishes.

Inniskillin Wines 1999 Chardonnay Founders' Reserve Chardonnay

Niagara Peninsula $$$ (558031)

A delicious mouthful of Chardonnay with toasted aromas and flavours and a soft, spicy mouth-feel. There's a pleasant creamy middle and end to this wine and a spicy apple note that gains richness, depth and nuance on the finish. Drink now to 2007.

Inniskillin Wines 1999 Chardonnay Reserve

Niagara Peninsula $ (317768)

One whiff and you're back in nana's kitchen waiting for the apple pie to cool. Brown sugar, baked apple, cinnamon, vanilla and applesauce aromas give you plenty of cause to keep your nose placed firmly in your glass for the better part of dinner. Alas, the palate isn't as complex, but there's a pleasant crisp green apple character that recalls Chablis at its racy best.

Jackson-Triggs Niagara Estate 2000 Proprietors' Reserve Chardonnay

Niagara Peninsula $ (526251)

This stellar value-priced Chardonnay has complexity and character far beyond its $10 price tag. The whiff and taste of roasted nuts, with butterscotch and smoke, add excitement to the solid core of apple and pear fruit. Subtle and supple, this is a dynamite food wine. Serve with smoked fish, grilled scallops, sweetbreads or game birds. Hosts take note: it comes in a 1.5-litre bottle for less than $20.

Lailey Vineyard 2000 Chardonnay Old Vines
Niagara Peninsula $$$$

The pungent citrus and oak aromas and concentrated polished fruit announce the arrival of a big-time Chardonnay. Citrus and oak carry over onto the palate, with a slightly honeyed note suspended over top. The finish is a little tart, which suggests pairing this wine with food for best enjoyment.

Lakeview Cellars 2000 Reserve Chardonnay
Niagara Peninsula $$$ (602557)

Serves up a tight, flinty beam of fruit, with citrus and mineral aromas and attractive ripe fruit notes unfolding after swirling the glass. Nice balance and finish. There's finesse here. Fans of complex flavours and higher acidity will take a shine to this reserve bottling.

Malivoire Wine Company 1999 Chardonnay Moira Vineyard
Niagara Peninsula $$$

Packs in a lot of complex flavours, with ripe pear, tropical fruit and a pretty array of smoky, toasty oak. It's crisp and clean, a polished mouthful of Chardonnay, finishing long and rich. Drink now through 2008.

Mission Hill Family Estate Winery 2000 Reserve Chardonnay
Okanagan Valley $$ (545004)

Stand back, this wine threatens to burst out of its glass. A huge pineapple nose dominates the intense aromatics, which feature the most curious and breathtaking rose note. It's one powerful wine that balances its high-octane alcohol content with a deep, rich concentration of flavours. Caution: do not open near a campfire.

Peller Estates 1999 Private Reserve Chardonnay Barrel-Aged

Niagara Peninsula $$ (981266)

A soft, floral Chardonnay that mixes apple, citrus and green pineapple fruit with complex orange blossom and toasted nut flavours. The palate is round and tasty, but lacks a keen focus. The flavours come across a little muddled.

Peninsula Ridge Estates Winery 2001 Inox Chardonnay

Niagara Peninsula $$ (594226)

Peninsula Ridge's unoaked Chardonnay ("inox" is French for stainless, referring to the fermentation tanks employed) puts the focus solely on the taste of the grape and, by extension, the taste of the soil. Delicate yet vivid floral, pear and some grassy aromas stir the senses. On the palate, it's a blend of round apple and pear notes with a slight nutty finish.

Peninsula Ridge Estates Winery 2000 Reserve Chardonnay

Niagara Peninsula $$$$

A serious, earthy Chardonnay with the kinds of aromas that folks either love or hate, such as wet cement and burnt popcorn. Rich and round, this wine has serious structure, mid intensity fruit and a long lovely finish. Not for everyone, but those who like it will drain the bottle when you're not looking.

Reif Estate Winery 1999 Chardonnay Reserve Estate

Niagara Peninsula $$ (252163)

Although it's a little disjointed right now, this wine has all the components of a crackerjack Chardonnay. Complex aromas of butter, cedar and creamy, subtle melon make for a great first impression. On the palate, the wine scores more points with its upfront fruit and zingy acidity. Although the oak is coming on too aggressively, this is a wine that's all set to go-go.

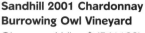

Sandhill 2001 Chardonnay
Burrowing Owl Vineyard
Okanagan Valley $ (541193)

The Burrowing Owl Vineyard produces some of British Columbia's best-quality wine, and this is no exception. Toast and tropical fruit aromas extend a most obliging welcome. The attractive palate is laced with sweet apple and rich round tropical fruit flavours. Spice and lime add balance and finesse. An excellent sipping wine.

Southbrook Winery 1999 Chardonnay
Lailey Vineyard
Niagara Peninsula $$ (448316)

The evocative aroma of baked, buttered apples and citrus is as enjoyable as an "E" ticket ride at Disneyland. The carnival ride continues as the rich, buttery liquid courses over your taste buds. This wine has got wonderful texture, but the flavour comes up short.

Southbrook Winery 1998 Chardonnay
Triomphe Chardonnay
Niagara Peninsula $$ (533315)

The nose points to a blockbuster Chardonnay with wafts of vanilla, banana and pear. The palate is equally big time, packed with ripe fruit, toasty oak and a lush, buttery texture. The weight is beautifully balanced by a bright acidity and lingering spicy note on the finish. Well done.

Stonechurch Vineyards 1999 St. David's
Bench Reserve Chardonnay
Niagara Peninsula $$ (569426)

Aromatic, with an appealing floral and Muscat note, this wine is extremely tasty by the glass. Fruit-driven, with complexity of lingering spice notes, Stonechurch's reserve has a creamy middle and finishes with a clean sweep of acidity. Well made.

Stoney Ridge Cellars 2000 Chardonnay Bench
Niagara Peninsula $ (292839)

A sterling wine that's a stand out on the price/ quality axis. Luscious fruit and vanilla aromas awaken your olfactories. There's also a unique floral note to this wine that'll keep your nose in the glass for a long time. On the palate, the peaches-and-cream texture dazzles your taste buds. Finely structured, the wine is strapped on to a high-octane alcohol content that fires up the fruit.

Strewn Wines 2000 Chardonnay French Oak Terroir
Niagara Peninsula $$ (618553)

One tasting note made it plain: "Holy Cow!" A tasty wine, with big buttered toast and smoke aromas and rich, ripe concentrated flavours. The palate is warm from the high alcohol content and it's got enough extraction to stand up to the added heat. A solid cellar candidate—lay down for two or three years and enjoy.

Sumac Ridge Estate Winery 2000 Chardonnay Private Reserve
Okanagan Valley $$ (393710)

A wine with obvious character and flair, this offers delicate muskmelon aromas and a richly extracted palate of ripe fruit flavours with a slightly sweet nut nuance. The creamy mouth-feel is refreshed by a balanced acidity. Best with food.

Thirty Bench Wines 1999 Chardonnay Reserve Steve Kocsis Vineyard
Niagara Peninsula $$$

Smouldering aromas—some yeasty, *sur lie* notes, matchstick, earth and caramel—had some panelists scratching their heads. It's distinctive alright, but is it good? The palate posed no such dilemma. Butter and tropical fruit, full, round texture and some lingering spicy notes. It's all good.

Vineland Estates Winery 2000 Chardonnay

Niagara Peninsula $ (191635)

Lighter and more delicate than many of its 2000 counterparts, Vineland Estates Chardonnay doesn't give any quarter when it comes to drinking pleasure. A fruit-forward wine, boasting plenty of lush banana and pear fruit packed onto its lithe frame, this is a solid sipping wine and excellent dinner companion. Serve with grilled veal chops, pork tenderloin medallions, game birds or pan-roasted sea bass or salmon. Be sure to have another bottle on hand. You'll need it.

Willow Heights 1999 Chardonnay Stefanik Vineyard Reserve

Niagara Peninsula $$ (487025)

A marvel for its creamy mouth-feel and fleshy core of ripe fruit, this is Chardonnay at its most sensual. Toasty aromas and flavours and some floral notes add a seductive hint. The palate has a touch of residual sweetness and a long, lingering finish that will curl your toes.

QUITE GOOD

Château des Charmes Winery 2000 Chardonnay Estate

Niagara Peninsula $ (081653)

In the words of one panelist: "Naked Chardonnay." Peaches and cream on the palate with a subtle spicy note. Nicely polished fruit. Drink now, with or without a meal.

Château des Charmes Winery 1998 Chardonnay St. Davids Bench Vineyard

Niagara Peninsula $$ (430991)

An elegant wine with class and character, this is an earthy Burgundian model of Chardonnay, packaged with ripe fruit and nutty flavours and a refreshing mineral character. This single-vineyard wine would be a serious, thoughtful dinner companion.

Colio Estate Vineyards 2000 CEV Chardonnay Aged Without Oak

Niagara Peninsula $ (503383)

Lightly aromatic (almond, some violet) and modestly flavoured, this unoaked wine captures lemon-lime notes and some earthy green apple flavours. Not very Chardonnay-like, but a decent crisp white wine that would be refreshing on a hot day. Drink now.

Domaine Combret 1996 Chardonnay Reserve Estate Bottled

Okanagan Valley $ (358507)

Well-balanced, complex Chardonnay with herb and citrus notes and a firm mineral streak. The palate is punctuated with an intense acidity. This wine is lively and fresh despite its advanced age. Enjoy with seafood pastas and risottos or baked pasta stuffed with ricotta.

Featherstone Estate Winery 2000 Chardonnay Barrel Fermented

Niagara Peninsula $

Pleasant aromas of citrus, smoke and melon and a slightly sweet palate stand out in this crowd-pleasing Chardonnay. Enjoy by the glass or with vegetable skewers and grilled peppers.

Harbour Estates Winery 2000 Chardonnay Non-Oaked

Niagara Peninsula $

Delicious fruit, especially mango and pineapple, but not a lot of depth. Serve slightly chilled as an aperitif or have on hand for a Tuesday night bar-becue. This wine will match nicely with grilled pork chops, chicken or well-seasoned shrimp skewers.

Harvest Estate Wines 2000 Chardonnay Barrel Fermented

Niagara Peninsula $ (579938)

There's a hint of coconut and wet straw on the nose of this creamy model of Chardonnay. A couple of panelists suggested this could be a sleeper, a wine that will lose its surly edge and reveal an inner beauty. Here's hoping. Perhaps a kiss from a princess will speed things along.

Henry of Pelham Family Estate Winery 2000 Chardonnay Barrel Fermented

Niagara Peninsula $$ (268342)

Spice essences and a slight leesy note picked up from fermentation in small oak barrels form an inviting frame around the ripe fruit aromas and fresh acidity. It is extremely well made and should be a strong complement to grilled seafood and chicken.

Hillebrand Estates 2000 Chardonnay Collector's Choice Barrel Aged

Niagara Peninsula $$ (291682)

Some toast and tropical fruit stand out in this clean, well-made Chardonnay. The nose and palate were somewhat closed and subdued. Might be better given some time in the bottle to find its inner Chardonnay voice.

Hillebrand Estates 2000 Showcase Chardonnay Barrel 4099 (New Troncais Oak) Huebel Vineyard

Niagara Peninsula $$$ (980979)

Fat texture, soft and fleshy, this wine is simple though a bit raw right now. It ends on a high note, with a twang of toasty oak spice that wakes up your taste buds.

Hillebrand Estates 1997 Trius Chardonnay Beamsville Bench Barrel Fermented

Niagara Peninsula $$ (291468)

Good developing bouquet of ripe apple, clove and spice and notes of honey. On the palate, there's nice butterscotch, apple and a smooth, spicy oak finish. A solid choice for turkey with stuffing, shrimp or vegetable skewers or pasta with garlic cream sauce.

Jackson-Triggs Okanagan Estate 2000 Proprietors' Grand Reserve Chardonnay

Okanagan Valley $$ (572065)

Best for the pure fruit aromas—pear, pineapple, some anise—which are absolutely pukka, in the parlance of Jamie "the Naked Chef" Oliver. The fruit gets knocked aside by the overpowering peppery and warm alcohol character. Better with food, which will help temper that booze heat.

Kacaba Vineyards 2000 Chardonnay French Oak

Niagara Peninsula $$$$

Toasty vanilla notes spice up the nose and a hit of sweetness adds some interest to the palate of this well-crafted Chardonnay. Deep appley fruit and a nice bright acidity add to the enjoyment of this mouth-filling wine.

Kacaba Vineyards 1999 Chardonnay

Niagara Peninsula $$

Lots of complex oak nuances that overwhelm the fruit flavours. Serve with gamy meats and deep-sea fish and use that stiff wood to complement the rustic nature of your meal.

Lakeview Cellars 2000 Unoaked Chardonnay Cherry Hill Vineyard

Niagara Peninsula $ (602557)

Tasty melon and pear and some almond notes are featured in this soft, fruity Chardonnay. There's richness and a lower acidity. This could be a real sleeper that turns into a cracking good wine in a year or two.

Magnotta Wines 1999 Chardonnay Barrel Fermented

Niagara Peninsula $

A light, lean offering with an interesting cinnamon note lurking behind the pear and apple highlights. A quicksilver vein of acidity makes this a good match for anything in a cream sauce.

Malivoire Wine Company 2000 Chardonnay

Niagara Peninsula $$ (573147)

This is an earthy Old World variation on Chardonnay that split the panel. Complex leesy and deep toast notes mix with some citrus and apple fruit. The style's not for everyone, but fans of nutty, austere white Burgundy take note.

Marynissen Estates 2000 Chardonnay Barrel Fermented A Estate

Niagara Peninsula $$

Mild tobacco and pineapple aromas and nice lively fruit on the palate make for an enjoyable Chardonnay. Enjoy with white meat in a cream and chanterelle mushroom sauce.

Mission Hill Family Estate 2000 Chardonnay Bin 99

Okanagan Valley $ (518530)

Dried pineapple and ripe fruit aromas combine for an interesting nose. The fruit consumes the palate and blends with a pleasant vanilla note. Simple yet succulent.

Peller Estates 1999 Chardonnay
Andrew Peller Signature Series Sur Lie

Niagara Peninsula $$$ (981159)

The wine is much subtler than the price. Complex cedar and vanilla notes, and a soft, milky and buttery palate that is refreshed by the warm alcohol character.

Pillitteri Estates Winery 2001 Unoaked Chardonnay

Niagara Peninsula $

Simple and subtle wine with good acidity and positive fruit characteristics. It's elegant and simple. Just the thing for wedding dinners and other social functions where you've got to please a cast of thousands.

Quails' Gate Estate Winery 2000 Chardonnay Limited Release

Okanagan Valley $$ (377770)

Good fruit, especially tropical pineapple notes, but not a lot of depth here. Nicely balanced and clean. Good sipping wine or an excellent way to perk up crab or shellfish dishes.

Strewn Wines 1998 Chardonnay Terroir Strewn Vineyard

Niagara Peninsula $$ (542415)

A buttery wine with clean tropical fruit flavours and a firm backbone of oak smoke and toast. Butterscotch and banana flavours add some complexity.

Thirty Bench Wines 1999 Chardonnay Tradition

Niagara Peninsula $ (572149)

"Tradition" is code for unoaked, this despite the prominent oak barrel logo on the label. Confused? Welcome to the wonderful world of Thirty Bench. Interesting yeasty, spicy and tropical fruit notes. The wine is a bit flabby, but will please a wide variety of palates.

Thornhaven Estates 2000 Chardonnay
Okanagan Valley $ (724872)
A soft, creamy expression of Chardonnay, with good flavours and short, slightly bitter finish. Drink now.

GEWÜRZTRAMINER

Can you say Gewürztraminer? If you can—
and you aren't afraid to ask for it by name in a
restaurant—pat yourself on the back, you're in the
minority. Gewürztraminer (pronounced Ga-vertz-
trau-mee-ner) is a highly aromatic white wine with
an unfriendly consumer name. Bestowed a
German title based on the town, Tramin, in which
the grape was discovered and tagged with
"gewürz," which means spiced or perfumed in
German, Gewürztraminer has fought an uphill
public relations battle ever since.

Known around the *Vines* office as the G-wine—
simply because it's easier to say—Gewürztraminer
has been enjoying rising production in Canada.
Noted by its pink-skinned coat when it's ready to
harvest, the journey of the Gewürztraminer grape
starts with the acid levels. Requiring a cooler
growing season to reach the higher acidity levels

FOOD PAIRING SUGGESTIONS
It's commonly held that
Gewürztraminer is best
suited for spicy dishes,
but only if it's an off-dry
style with a slightly sweet
touch. Dry Gewürztraminer
would be better suited to
pork roast, stews and
casseroles. Also, for best
effect, always chill the
wine before serving. It
really enhances the
flavour profile. So order in
an array of Thai or Indian
dishes and invite a few
guests over for an
impromptu cultural
experience.

that establish the foundation of a well-made G-wine, the little grape that could appears to have found an ideal home in British Columbia and Ontario. With acid levels in check, it becomes the winemaker's task to extract the grape's true potential. A hallmark G-wine will be a deeply golden colour and have a very perfumed nose, with loads of ripe lychee fruit and soapy, rosewater characteristics. Ripe tropical fruits can also make an appearance. Other notable characteristics include a full body with a higher alcohol range than most whites.

When looking for a benchmark Gewürztraminer, Alsace would be the best place to start. The Alsatians have pioneered the varietal and are consistently producing beautiful Gewürztraminers. In Canada, the potential is definitely there. Winemakers in both British Columbia and Ontario have hit the target, but not on a consistent basis. The 2000 vintage in Ontario produced some wonderfully complex Gewürztraminers. "The key to producing a Gewürztraminer of such classic style in the 2000 vintage was the warm and sunny autumn conditions coupled with the later-than-usual harvest date (October 14, 2000). The wine's distinctive character is the direct result of the unique terroir of our St. Davids Bench vineyard," commented Paul A. Bosc of Château des Charmes Winery in Niagara. Wineries in British Columbia followed suit with some glowing examples of well-made Gewürztraminer from the 2001 vintage, which by all accounts provided ideal conditions for producing great wines from later-ripening grapes. Once consistency has been established, Canada will become known for its delicious Gewürztraminer.

Tasting Panel: SP, RW, SS, LC, CR, WS, CW

VINES AWARD

Château des Charmes Winery 2000 Gewürztraminer St. Davids Bench Vineyard

Niagara Peninsula $ (453472)

Unlike last year's guide, in which there were no benchmark G-wines, this year sees Château des Charmes coming out with a classic that captures all that is good about Gewürztraminer. Built in an Alsatian style, its fragrance is full of fresh rose petal, ripe lychee and nutmeg. On the palate, the pleasing scents give way to a deep, textured wine without missing a beat. A slightly oily texture with a racy streak accents the lychee and ginger flavours, and a spicy finish caps this wonderful wine. Best enjoyed while watching *East Meets West* with Ming Tsai or with your favourite spicy Asian cuisine.

HIGHLY RECOMMENDED

Cave Spring Cellars 2000 Gewürztraminer

Niagara Peninsula $ (302059)

When Cave Spring released its 1997 G-wine it set a benchmark for the wine in Niagara. Aromatically intense with lychee, minerals and a thin floral line, the 2000 offering is the closest they have come to replicating that stellar vintage. On the palate, the complexity of the wine really starts to work, with multiple layers of fruit and texture. A crisp acidity is rounded out on the mid palate by a viscous presence that enhances the spicy character of the fruit flavours. A classic Gewürztraminer, both graceful and expressive, like actress Juliette Binoche in *Chocolat*.

Domaine de Chaberton Estates 2001 Gewürztraminer

Fraser Valley $ (714261)

Although this wine had some panelists claiming a Riesling invader, it has the markings of a sophisticated Gewürztraminer. Notes of lemon, lychee and even a hint of cinnamon offer an intriguing introduction to the wine. On the palate, it's a spicy blend of citrus, pepper and grassy flavours. Enjoy this intense, lively wine with cocktails, or just chill it down and kick back with jazz sensation Jane Bunnett playing in the background.

Mission Hill Family Estate Winery 2001 Gewürztraminer

Okanagan Valley $ (524587)

Winemaker John Simes has developed quite a knack for producing consistently tasty Gewürztraminer. Typical notes of lemon and lanolin are blended with an interesting hint of grass. A great line of acidity heightens the flavour intensity on the palate. A dash of spice on the finish caps a versatile wine that would make a great match for Thai food or seasoned pork roast.

Reif Estate Winery 2000 Gewürztraminer Semi-Dry

Niagara Peninsula $

Made in the style of a German Gewürztraminer, this wine has more residual sugar than most others in the tasting. The added touch of sweetness enhances the flavour profiles of ripe pineapple, lychee and peach. A pronounced oily texture on the palate balances the acidity, giving the wine a depth of character that is often lacking in other Canadian G-wines. Having left the grapes to hang on the vine to ripen beyond when most wineries harvest, Reif has managed to create a versatile wine with all the markings of a classic Gewürztraminer. Spicy Thai or Indian dishes would be a great match.

Sumac Ridge Estate Winery 2000 Gewürztraminer Private Reserve

Okanagan Valley $ (142893)

If there's one wine that Sumac always manages to nail, it's Gewürztraminer. Year after year, winemaker Mark Wendenberg crafts intensely tasty G-wines. The 2000 offering has a fragrant nose of rose, ginger and apple. On the palate, delicious flavours of grapefruit, lychee and spice are elevated by bright acidity. A racy finish caps this finely made wine. Pair with Mexican dishes.

Thornhaven Estates 2001 Gewürztraminer

Okanagan Valley $ (731661)

The first release from one of the Okanagan's newly minted wineries, this great G-wine is hopefully a sign of a tasty future for Thornhaven. A tropical fruit explosion greets the nose with a wash of peach, grapefruit and a hint of rosewater. A robust acidity enhances the tropical fruit flavours. An attractive oily texture adds a depth to the wine that makes it worthy of a five-alarm fire code on the Thai menu.

Wild Goose Vineyards 2001 Gewürztraminer

Okanagan Valley $ (414748)

A delightfully delicious wine that turns on the water taps in the mouth. Chalk full of ripe lychee with a nice floral undertone of rose and anise. The intensity continues on the palate with layers of fruit and spice. A great balance of acidity carries the wine to the finish with an added touch of hot spice. A regular highlight in G-wine tastings, Wild Goose continues to show why it's one of the top wineries in British Columbia. Pairing partners would be spiced freshwater fish such as trout or oven-roasted Cajun chicken.

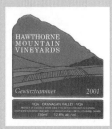

RECOMMENDED

Hawthorne Mountain Vineyards 2001 Gewürztraminer

Okanagan Valley $ (440685)

Winemaker Bruce Ewert is another artisan of fine Gewürztraminer in the Valley. Unmistakable fragrances of peach blossoms and violets are blended together with ripe lychee and spice to create an appealing aroma. Boosted flavours of lychee and grapefruit wash over the palate. The perfect sidekick to curry-infused Indian dishes.

Jackson-Triggs Niagara Estate 2000 Proprietors' Reserve Gewürztraminer

Niagara Peninsula $ (526269)

One sniff and you'll know you're in G-wine land with big notes of lychee, peach and apricot. Ripe, rich flavours of grapefruit, lime and peach with a touch of allspice are held together by a fine line of acidity. Built in a semi-dry style, there's just the right amount of residual sugar to enhance the fruit without making it too intrusive. The crisp finish refreshes the palate, making a perfect match for spicy dishes. A great buy that would make it an easy choice with take-out Asian dishes.

Lakeview Cellars 2000 Gewürztraminer Butler's Grant Vineyard

Niagara Peninsula $ (535625)

An attractively perfumed wine that captures the classic notes of Gewürztraminer with soft notes of pear, lychee nut, pineapple and ginger. Designed to be off-dry, it has enough acidity to create a nice oily texture with the residual sugar. Fuller in body, the ripe fruit carries through to an elegant finish. Try with pork chops and spicy mashed potatoes.

Konzelmann Estate Winery 2000 Gewürztraminer Late Harvest Winemaster's Collection

Niagara Peninsula $ (200550)

This premium level wine from Konzelmann is produced with grapes specially selected during harvest. As with the 1999 offering, the selected grapes have been allowed to ripen an extra few weeks on the vine and it shows in the bottle. A perfumed nose of allspice and dried orange peel. Fuller bodied on the palate, it has enough acidity to carry the robust flavours through to a spicy finish.

Konzelmann Estate Winery 1999 Gewürztraminer (Late Harvest)

Niagara Peninsula $ (392357)

Although the label says "late harvest," it's not a late harvest wine in the sugar code sense. Built to be dry, this wine's reference to late harvest relates to the extra hanging time the grapes had on the vine. Much like typical Alsatian Gewürztraminers, the additional few weeks of ripening intensified the flavours of lychee, pine-apple and peach. A viscous texture on the palate adds complexity with just the right amount of acidity. A spicy finish rounds out this wonderfully made wine.

Quails' Gate Estate Winery 2001 Gewürztraminer Limited Release

Okanagan Valley $ (585745)

This off-dry G-wine is the perfect tonic after a long day at the office. Intense aromas of ripe lychee, melon and pineapple awaken the senses. A fruit explosion in the mouth, with just the right amount of residual sugar to make this a deliciously thirst-quenching wine. Loosen the tie, kick off the shoes, uncork and unwind with a plate of cheese.

St. Hubertus Estate Winery 2001 Oak Bay Vineyard Gewürztraminer

Okanagan Valley $ (597229)

Hallmark aromatics of lychee, rosewater and a dash of ginger. Racy acidity lifts the fruit flavours over the palate through to a crisp, clean finish. It's like the actor Kevin Klein—he elevates the film with his talents, but few people can remember his role.

Vineland Estates Winery 2000 Gewürztraminer

Niagara Peninsula $ (434779)

A stalwart producer of crisp, clean whites, Vineland continues to uphold its fine reputation with this 2000 offering. Elegant in design, the wine has subtle notes of lychee nut, apricot and melon with a soft touch of lemon. Its flavour profile is spicier, with ginger and nutmeg providing a racy nuance to the lush fruit. It's like the novel *Snow Falling on Cedars*—it grows on you without your really noticing, and you can't seem to put it down.

Vineland Estates Winery 1999 Frontier Vineyard Reserve Gewürztraminer

Niagara Peninsula $$

Like a three-year racing horse just starting to hit its stride, this reserve Gewürztraminer is evolving into a more mature white. Spicy notes of ginger and allspice are more pronounced, with mellow fruit notes of papaya and melon. A textured, oily mouth-feel enhances the spicy flavours and allows the fruit to glide over the palate through to the finish. Off-dry in style, this would be very enjoyable with mildly spiced Asian fusion dishes.

QUITE GOOD

Creekside Estate Winery 2001 Gewürztraminer

Niagara Peninsula $ (593640)

Lots of upfront tropical fruit with pineapple and apricot. On the lighter side on the palate, it's all fruit. A small dash of spice on the finish rounds out the wine. A good wine to keep in the fridge to enhance those late-night cheese cravings.

Featherstone Estate Winery 2001 Gewürztraminer

Niagara Peninsula $

A good debut vintage from a new bench winery in Niagara. Classic in style, it has all the elements of a well-made Gewürztraminer. It's off-dry in style, with enough lychee, ginger and lemon flavours to make for a refreshing white. A nutty profile competes with the fruit, but a zesty finish makes it a versatile wine for all your spicy cravings.

Harbour Estates Winery 2000 Gewürztraminer

Niagara Peninsula $

Fruit forward with apple and melon notes dominating, this flavourful wine is crisp, clean and well constructed. Although it doesn't come across as a G-wine, it's still delicious enough to be served at the family picnic.

Henry of Pelham Family Estate Winery 2000 Gewürztraminer

Niagara Peninsula $ (268359)

A soft and supple Gewürztraminer that doesn't overpower the senses, but provides just the right amount of character to match perfectly with Muenster cheese, liver pâtés and smoked salmon. There are subtle grapefruit, lanolin and spicy flavours with a lighter acidity. Ideal wine for a larger social gathering.

Hillside Estate 2001 Gewürztraminer
Okanagan Valley $ (505206)
Definitely a patio wine. Pink grapefruit, lemon and pineapple aromas are accentuated on the palate by a touch of sweetness. Its less intrusive acidity makes for easy sipping. Chill, uncork and unwind.

Reif Estate Winery 2001 Gewürztraminer
Niagara Peninsula $
A reserved wine that spreads its wings on the palate. Soft peach and pineapple flavours gently roll over the tongue towards a fruit finish. A weighty wine that needs some spicy food to help smooth out the edges.

Strewn Wines 1999 Gewürztraminer
Niagara Peninsula $ (576017)
A mellow wine that comes alive after a while in the glass. Spice flavours of ginger and allspice dominate, with soft flavours of apricot. Subtle spicy finish could be matched with pad Thai or smoked salmon.

PINOT BLANC

Considered a mutant of the Pinot Noir family, Pinot Blanc is so far removed from the grape's family tree that it was adopted by the Chardonnay family for many years and called Pinot Chardonnay. Talk about no respect. A fringe varietal not widely pro-duced on the world stage, Pinot Blanc has been taken up by some Canadian wineries in an effort to make it a wine favourite. Winemakers favour this grape because of its habit of early ripening as well as its vigorous and productive capabilities. Although not overtly aromatic, its frequently high acidity and full body allow many producers to design the wine to be consumed with food.

This year's tasting panel had an interesting scenario—after tasting through all the wines, the panel did a re-taste of the wines that received highly recommended marks. With just under half the wines in the tasting receiving high marks, a

FOOD PAIRING SUGGESTIONS
Depends on the wine-making style. Unoaked Pinot Blanc can be paired with spicy foods such as Asian cuisine, grilled vegetables and steamed shellfish. Oaked offerings would go well with smoked fish, pork roast and other lean meats.

comment was made about the great progress from last year's tasting to this year. Across the board, the wines showed much more character and complexity. Strewn Wines winemaker Joe Will indicated that the acids in 2000 were higher than usual, and after a year in the bottle, many of the wines were starting to shine. According to Matthias Boss, winemaker at Konzelmann Estate Winery, "the year 2000 was a perfect growing season for the early-ripening Pinot Blanc."

The 2001s were increasingly more fruit forward, with Pinot Blancs from the Okanagan Valley really demonstrating a knack for being well-balanced, delicious offerings. "We have always had a great admiration for Pinot Blanc in the Okanagan Valley," explained Roland Kruger, wine-maker at Wild Goose Vineyards. "It grows so well in the Okanagan and provides excellent fruit qualities after the wine is fermented. It maintains good acid and ripening qualities in the vineyard. It is another one of those varieties that does not garner a lot of respect from the consumer (just like Riesling)."

Tasting Panel: SS, JW, WS, CW

VINES AWARD

Konzelmann Estate Winery 2000 Pinot Blanc
Niagara Peninsula $ (219279)

Modeled after Pinot Blanc from Alsace, France, this award-winner is all about balance. Like the great tightrope walker, Jean François Gravelet, The Great Blondin, who balanced his way across Niagara Falls in 1859, winemaker Herbert Konzelmann does a magnificent job of keeping this wine together. Plenty of unctuous fruit such as passion fruit, peach and pineapple offer an enticing-enough entry, but it's in the mouth that this wine shines.

The rich fruit washes over the palate with a nice soft, but full acidity. The weight of the wine allows the fruit to carry well through to the finish. A well-made, superbly balanced dry wine. Try pork chops and grilled veggies with this wonderful white.

HIGHLY RECOMMENDED

CedarCreek Estate Winery 2000 Greata Ranch Vineyards Pinot Blanc
Okanagan Valley $$ (605253)
Aptly described by one panelist as "peaches and cream." A combination of tropical fruit and a touch of toasty oak gives this wine an added depth. A rush of ripe peaches and passion fruit on the nose gives way to a creamy peach and pineapple character on the palate. The oak provides the wine with a round, supple softness that plays well off the acidity. Could be mistaken for a Chardonnay, and if you're tired of Chards, seek this one out and let it ride with smoked salmon or pork roast.

Hester Creek Estate Winery 1999 Pinot Blanc
Okanagan Valley $ (467316)
Highly aromatic with ripe melon, peach blossom and even lychee nut creating an attractive fragrance. The intense fruit carries over to the palate with a quick hit of sweetness on the front and a racy acidity on the finish. It's like Michael Keaton in *Pacific Heights*—seems sweet, but has a mean streak as well. Great for picnics and garden parties.

Sumac Ridge Estate Winery 2000 Pinot Blanc Private Reserve

Okanagan Valley $ (393728)

This oaked offering captures the essence of Pinot Blanc with the added complexity of wood. There's enough fruit intensity, with pear, grapefruit and lemon, to not be overpowered by oak. A thin layer of toasty vanilla coats the fruit, providing a softness to the acidity. A spicy finish caps off a great white. Built for the cuisine of the West Coast, this wine would pair well with smoked or grilled seafood and grilled white meats.

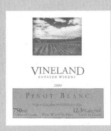

Vineland Estates Winery 2000 Pinot Blanc

Niagara Peninsula $ (563478)

The runner-up to the *Vines* Award, this wine has really developed within the past year. A "quite good" ranking last year was due to high levels of acidity that knocked the fruit around in the mouth. Now, the wine is showing exceptionally well. Anise, lemon and passion fruit aromas foreshadow what's to come on the palate. Loads of tropical fruit—think melon, pineapple and citrus—dance around in the mouth with flavours held together by a soft but defined layer of acidity. Zippy and zesty capture the mood of this crisp, clean, refreshing Pinot Blanc. An ideal sipping wine on the patio or with a fresh seafood platter.

Wild Goose Vineyards 2001 Pinot Blanc

Okanagan Valley $ (414722)

Talk about getting ready to go on a date. This one has a highly attractive perfumed aroma. Although it could be mistaken for a Gewürztraminer with its ripe lychee notes, there are also hints of peach and passion fruit that give the wine one of the best fragrances of the entire tasting. The intense fruit continues on the palate with streaks of acidity that carry the wine well through to the finish. Complex yet elegant, like Sara Jessica Parker in *Sex and the City*.

RECOMMENDED

Mission Hill Family Estate 2000 Pinot Blanc
Okanagan Valley $ (300301)
Like John Woo's *Face/Off* starring Nicolas Cage
and John Travolta, this wine has two faces. It had
some panelists thinking Sauvignon Blanc with its
intense grass and lemon notes. Yet flavours are
consistent with a warm-region Pinot Blanc with its
high acidity and intense citrus and pineapple
characteristics. Best enjoyed with spicy Asian
dishes, as the clean, crisp, slightly hot finish will
cleanse the palate before the next bite of food.

Strewn Wines 1999 Pinot Blanc
Niagara Peninsula $ (522748)
A one-two offering where the oak tends to dominate. Immediate toasty aromas cloak the light
tropical fruit notes, but after the initial splash of
oak on the palate, peach and melon emerge with
a crest of acidity. A medium-bodied white with
enough depth to match most white meats, lighter
cheeses or linguine with sautéed shrimp.

QUITE GOOD

Mission Hill Family Estate 2001 Pinot Blanc
Okanagan Valley $ (300301)
Zesty lemon would be the best description for
this citrus delight. Intense lemon from the nose
to the palate is enhanced by a strong thread
of acidity that runs from top to bottom. Well
integrated, this crisp, clean white would be best
enjoyed chilled on the patio or as a cocktail
before dinner.

Sumac Ridge Estate Winery 2000 Pinot Blanc
Okanagan Valley $ (327882)
A lighter-oaked offering than Sumac's Private Reserve Pinot Blanc, this one is like the shy sibling who opens up when the others aren't around. Lightly toasted with pear and pineapple, it has enough fruit to make it a summer sipper, and just enough toasty oak to go with a meal. Best suited for the picnic basket with a tuna salad or smoked turkey club sandwiches.

PINOT GRIS

For many wine lovers, Pinot Gris is like the cousin you've always heard the family talk about but never got the chance to meet. You know, Cousin Larry, a successful something-or-other who lives in a town far away. You get the odd Christmas card from him, but that's about it.

In fact, Pinot Gris just happens to be a distant cousin of the popular Pinot Noir grape family; thus the name Pinot Gris, from its greyish-blue or brownish-pink skin. And if the Pinot Gris happens to reside in Italy or is made by an Italian-born producer, it becomes Pinot Grigio.

Pinot Gris can be made light and spritzy (usually the Pinot Grigio side of the fence) or rich and oily (hello, card-carrying Pinot Gris), depending on the winemaker and vintage. Neither style is overtly aromatic and, when looking for a well-made Pinot

FOOD PAIRING SUGGESTIONS
Not too sweet or flowery, Pinot Gris is perfect for fish (both fresh and salt-water), oysters and other shellfish—and any dish with flavours that benefit from the addition of lemon or lime. The acidity and ample fruit of Canadian Pinot Gris make it a match with spicy foods—think Indian, Asian and Middle Eastern cuisine.

Gris, you'll find the levels of extract and acidity are what can make or break this wine.

Frank Supernak, winemaker at B.C.'s Hester Creek Estate Winery, crafted his *Vines* Award winner with a cool ferment, which retains the great fruit character. Forty per cent was aged in older barrels to add a subtle butterscotch and vanilla complexity to the finished wine. "Pinot Gris is to the wine industry what Merlot was five years ago: the hottest varietal, with more and more plantings going into production every year," Supernak said. "Pinot Gris has much more finesse than Pinot Blanc. More perfume and mouth-feel as well."

In Canada, Pinot Gris is the new kid on the block that everyone wants to play with. The varietal is too young to have a clear-cut bench-mark. At present, winemakers are not making lighter Pinot Grigio–style wines—the wines are too flavourful and complex to be confused with those lean and light Italian numbers. But they're not concentrated and honeyed enough to rank as Tokay–Pinot Gris from Alsace.

Indeed, most wines in this tasting landed somewhere in the middle of that axis, with two distinct schools of winemaking: oak-aged wines refined by malolactic fermentation and crisp, clean products forged strictly in stainless tanks to amplify the intensity of the fruit flavours. With the varying wines came some great and not-so-great results. There's a lot of potential for Pinot Gris in Ontario and British Columbia, but winemakers need to focus their approach.

Tasting Panel: TK, SS, WS, CW, JW

VINES AWARD

Hester Creek Estate Winery 2000 Pinot Gris

Okanagan Valley $ (560037)

If this *Vines* Award winner were a piece of music, it would be a song by the ubiquitous techno-wizard Moby. You might never have heard of Moby, but it's almost certain you've heard his shapeshifting music. It's everywhere: on film soundtracks and the radio and hawking products such as VW cars and cell phones. It's hip yet engaging to people from all walks of life. Hester Creek's 2000 crowd-pleasing wine delivers lovely pear and citrus aromas, especially orange and tangerine notes. The delicious fruit character carries over onto the palate, which is full and rich in nature and had panelists tripping over themselves searching for praiseworthy adjectives. Sublime! Astonishing! Heavenly! Spectacular! Take your pick. Oak aging has added some complexity to this vibrant white, but not at the expense of the pure fruit flavours.

HIGHLY RECOMMENDED

Mission Hill Family Estate 2001 Pinot Grigio

Okanagan Valley $ (563981)

This stylish wine from Mission Hill was runner-up for the *Vines* Award. A delicious offering with good crisp character and engaging lemon zest and elderflower aromas, it is rounded out by deep, delicious spice and smoke flavours. An extremely well-made wine with excellent flavour and intensity, it finishes with a kiss of concentrated lemon peel flavour. This is a wine that's going to inspire the diehards to start an online fan club: www.greatgrigio.com.

Mission Hill Family Estate 2000 Pinot Gris
Okanagan Valley $ (563981)
Move over P. Diddy, Mission Hill has unleashed a cooler cat on the town: P. Gris. Cool enough to win over Jennifer Lopez and club kids across North America, this resonant white wine has good intensity and mouth-feel, making it a delicious and refreshing sipping wine. It also boasts good varietal character—those bright tropical fruit flavours are tempered with a quicksilver acidity and a flinty mineral streak that cuts across the palate. This excellent all-round wine will cause a commotion on the picnic blanket, on the back deck or in the stuffiest of formal dining settings. Well done.

Vineland Estates Winery 2000 Pinot Gris
Niagara Peninsula $$ (563460)
This wine exhibits the pinkish hue you should expect to see in quality Pinot Gris. Contact with the grape skins gives the wine a subtle colouring, adding some complexity to the wine's flavours and volume to its mouth-feel. Lemon tea, citrus and tropical fruit aromas command attention. Soft fruit flavours and a slight sweetness add to the enjoyment. This crowd-pleasing style of Pinot Gris is delicate enough to pair harmoniously with dinner but is rich and flavourful, too. Pleasant by the glass or with your favourite grilled fish served with salsa verde.

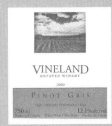

Wild Goose Vineyards 2001 Pinot Gris
Okanagan Valley $ (536227)
Here's a wine created in the Alsatian model: lovely lanolin aromas and an oily mouth-feel tweak a decidedly French strain of Pinot Gris. But the high-intensity aromas and ripe peach fruit flavours had panelists thinking Gewürztraminer instead of card-carrying Gris. It might not be a benchmark model of this varietal, but this is a complex and delicious wine that delighted panelists—as it will likely delight all fans of rich and fruity white wines. A perfect accompaniment to grilled fish and poultry with creamy sauces or a modest cheese plate, this wine also has enough fat and fruit to be enjoyed by itself as a pre-dinner apéritif.

RECOMMENDED

Blue Mountain 1999 Pinot Gris
Okanagan Valley $$ (329458)
This is a winemaker's take on Pinot Gris. The delicate fruit flavours have been enhanced by artful use of oak and extracted flavours from skin contact and barrel aging. Intense aromas and spicy citrus flavours delight. But the intensity and finish are a little muted. This medium-bodied wine will be a great companion for a family picnic or quiet time with Richard B. Wright's award-winning novel, *Clara Callan*.

Creekside Estate Winery 2001 Pinot Gris
Niagara Peninsula $
Deep and correct aromatics—smoke, almond and citrus lemon fruit—and a generous, round structure are the best attributes of this vibrant white. The flavours are simple, but linger on the palate. This is a wine to kick back and relax with.

Domaine de Chaberton Estates Limited 2001 Pinot Gris
Okanagan Valley $ (627638)
The aromas are enough to evoke rapturous tasting notes: intensely smoky, nutty, loads of tropical fruit and even fresh dates were some of the descriptors offered by panelists. The flavours aren't as pervasive, but there's some nice spice character lingering in the mix of this crisp, fresh white. The finish offers a blast of intense lime flavour, but it disappears too quickly. Another wine to enjoy on the patio, its charms are as fleeting as a Canadian summer.

Glenterra Vineyards 2000 Pinot Gris
Vancouver Island $$ (726109)
The aromas suggest lemon meringue pie, smoke and almond biscotti. On the palate, the flavours turn candied—lemon lollipop dominates in this crisp, clean wine. With its refreshing racy style, this Pinot Gris is an extremely versatile food wine.

Hawthorne Mountain Vineyards 2000 Pinot Gris
Okanagan Valley $$ (704999)
Subtle citrus and melon aromas combine with bright lemon flavours in this full-flavoured wine. Lower acidity makes it soft and a little flabby on the palate, but the flavours are so appealing and the finish offers such pleasant fruit notes that the panel was beguiled. This juicy wine would be perfect as an aperitif and has the right character to partner with spicy Indian or Thai dishes.

Mission Hill Family Estate 2001 Pinot Gris Reserve

Okanagan Valley $$ (537076)

The prominent pineapple and tropical fruit flavours and aromas struck most tasters as being more Pinot Blanc than Pinot Gris. Ripe fruit and bright intensity are the hallmarks of this tasty white, which will make friends easily and often. This is an excellent choice for large functions and family gatherings. It's complex enough to please the oenophiles and flavourful enough for those who could care less about good taste, but just want a glass of wine that tastes good.

Mission Hill Family Estate 2000 Pinot Gris Reserve

Okanagan Valley $$ (537076)

Full, round and complex, this Pinot Gris strikes a nice balance between fruit essence and deep honeysuckle and nutty flavours common to this grape varietal. Balanced, intense and complex, with a pleasant burst of tropical fruit aromas on the nose, this wine makes an excellent dinner companion.

Mission Hill Family Estate 1999 Pinot Gris Reserve

Okanagan Valley $$ (537076)

A touch of almond aroma adds complexity to this fresh, clean wine. A hint of pear fruit graces the palate, but the flavour profile offers a range of nutty and toasted flavours. It's a dry wine with good extracted flavours and a nice intensity that needs food to be at its best.

Pillitteri Estates Winery 2001 Pinot Grigio
Niagara Peninsula $ (349183)

This is an expression of Pinot Gris as femme fatale: a wine with smoky, mineral notes, a wine with an aura of mystery about it. It's not for everyone, but those who fall for its charms will fall hard. Toasted almond and some mineral aromas smoulder in the glass. On the palate, there's a hint of tangerine and lemon fruit that perks up the bitter nut and slightly flinty flavours. This is a wine made to pair with oysters and other shellfish.

QUITE GOOD

Cilento Wines 2001 Pinot Gris
Niagara Peninsula $

The decidedly pink colour had the panel thinking this wine made a wrong turn en route to the rosé tasting. It's clearly labelled as Pinot Gris, but what's in the bottle might have you scratching your head. The flavours don't match the colour or the flavour profile of Pinot Gris. It is, however, an enjoyable, aromatic wine with a nice balance of sweet and sour.

Colio Estate Vineyards 2000 Pinot Grigio CEV
Lake Erie North Shore $ (503391)

This barrel-aged wine has positive tropical fruit and almond aromas that are brought down to earth with a yeasty note that ruined the wine for some tasters. On the palate, it's soft and round, with enough stuffing to stand up to roast chicken or pork.

Hillebrand Estates 2000 Pinot Gris Vineyard Select

Niagara Peninsula $ (306894)

This wine's *SweetTart* aromas will take you back to the corner store, circa 1977. Candied fruit notes mingle with some spice and almond aromas that carry over onto the palate. This is a simple yet enjoyable wine with a nice long finish. Flavourful enough to sip by itself, dry enough to serve with dinner, it's an honest wine at a good price.

Inniskillin Wines 2001 Pinot Grigio

Niagara Peninsula $ (348979)

Inniskillin's light, simple take on Pinot Grigio leans towards the Italian benchmark. Nice tropical fruit flavours and bright acidity make for a balanced attack on the palate. Drink now.

Lakeview Cellars 2000 Pinot Gris

Niagara Peninsula $ (330464)

Lemon and nut aromas are followed closely by toasty, grassy flavours on the palate. The flavours run towards the bitter fruit and nut spectrum, which split the panel. Some thought the extracted flavours a sign of varietal character and complexity. Others demanded, "Where's the fruit?" The slightest hint of ripe fruit flavour would have vaulted this Gris into the big time.

Magnotta Wines 2000 Pinot Gris

Niagara Peninsula $

Apple and almond aromas turn smoky the longer this straw-coloured white lingers in the glass. On the palate, it's smooth, with pleasant honeydew and apple flavours and a crisp finish. This would be an interesting wine to serve during an afternoon wedding reception.

Thomas and Vaughan Vintners 2001 Pinot Gris
Niagara Peninsula $

An earthy take on Pinot Gris, with high-intensity aromatics of almond, smoke and flinty minerals. Zesty fruit (mostly grapefruit flavours) peaks out behind the round, full-bodied palate. This wine has enough fat to serve as an aperitif, but would also make for a good second mate to a poached fish dish.

Tinhorn Creek Vineyards 2001 Pinot Gris
Okanagan Valley $ (530683)

A hint of oak and some yeasty character add complexity to this straightforward wine. It's well made, with nice structure and intensity, but lacks the focussed fruit flavours that would round out the package. This is an excellent oyster wine.

RIESLING

If you want definitive proof that wine writers have minimal influence on wine trends, look no further than Riesling. Writers of purple-stained prose love it so much, they often become zealous missionaries trying to convert the world to the steely wine that, in its prime, offers orchard-fresh fruit and a live wire of acidity in every glass. Consumers, meanwhile, are continually nonplussed.

Year after year, with dogged determination and eternal optimism, the articles arrive with screaming headlines: The Rise of Riesling! Riesling's Revenge! Save Your Soul, Stop Drinking Chardonnay! It makes otherwise civilized and urbane minds sound like the drooling Brother John character in the Bugs Bunny cartoon, *Rabbit Hood.* "D'uh, don't you worry, never fear, Robin Hood will soon be here ..."

Pity poor Riesling. The world's noble white wine grape seems destined to live forever in the shadow

FOOD PAIRING SUGGESTIONS
Dry Rieslings are the most versatile white wines on the market for matching with cuisines as diverse as Thai, French, Mexican and California fusion. They also go well with appetizers, fried foods, freshwater and saltwater fish, pasta, stir-fries and salads, particularly dishes with citrus flavours. Off-dry styles are excellent sipping or apertif wines.

of easy-to-drink, easy-to-pronounce Chardonnay. The pride of Germany, Riesling is an agreeable drink that's all about the balance of fruit and acidity in the finished wine.

Unlike the prima donna Chardonnay, there's no performance-enhancing oak aging, no special additional fermentation to soften the wine or mellow its expressive flavours. Riesling is a down-to-earth, low-maintenance kind of wine. What you see in the grape is what you get in the glass.

Transplanted to any wine region of the world, it will reflect the unique soil and microclimate of the site, yet remain unequivocally Riesling. Its identity is bulletproof. In Canada, it performs exceptionally well, and winemakers are able to consistently produce wines that range from bone-dry to opulent and sweet. We're interested in drier styles here; the sweeter dessert wines are featured later in the book.

A highly aromatic wine, which offers predominantly citrus, lime and floral notes in British Columbia and Ontario vintages, Riesling develops more of a characteristic kerosene/petrol note as it ages. While Riesling has the capacity to cellar for a long time, most consumers enjoy the young-fruit characteristics of the wine as opposed to its aged grease-monkey notes.

For consumers, the upside to Riesling's second-class-citizen status means savvy wine shoppers have their pick of value-priced wines. On a value-for-money axis, it doesn't get any better than undervalued Rieslings, which generally retail in the eight to twelve dollar range.

From his vantage, Brian Schmidt, winemaker at Niagara-based Riesling specialist Vineland Estates, quality Riesling is traced back to its vineyard. Given its history, Vineland Estates has a sterling pedigree for Riesling. It was founded by German winemaker and nurseryman Hermann Weis, the man behind Mosel producer St. Urbans-Hof. After travelling to Washington State and British Columbia, Weis proclaimed the Niagara Bench to be ground zero for the New World Riesling revolution.

"I continually thank Hermann for the foresight," said Schmidt, whose 2000 Dry Riesling earned a five-star rating. Riesling is harder to produce than Chardonnay, which can be crafted and redefined by oak aging and secondary malolactic fermentation. Schmidt explained that vineyard siting and cool fermentation are the keys to crafting world-class Riesling. Vineyard sites are crucial because the wine is made on the vine; press the fruit and get out of the way. And cool fermentation helps retain the wine's fruit intensity and flavour.

The best of these wines can stand shoulder to shoulder with any Riesling imported into this country. This is a variety we do exceptionally well in both Ontario and British Columbia—and, not resting on their laurels, our winemakers continue to ratchet up the quality and finesse of these sublime wines.

Tasting Panel: AA, RC, AP, GP, WS, CW, JW

VINES AWARD

Vineland Estates Winery 2000 Dry Riesling
Niagara Peninsula $ (167551)
When confronted with an incredibly flavourful wine or meal, Berliners of a certain age can be heard to exclaim: "It's like an angel peed on my tongue!" This wine brought out the old Berliner in each panelist. It is bliss in a glass—let the record show, we said BLISS in a glass. Grapefruit and lime aromas introduce this firm, dry white. Peach and citrus flavours, with a slightly flinty mineral note, ride a wave of zesty acidity to a long, long finish. Drink or hold. Best from 2003 through 2008.

HIGHLY RECOMMENDED

Cave Spring Cellars 2000 Dry Riesling
Niagara Peninsula $ (233635)
Mineral characteristics and bright lime aromas are the calling card of this dry and sinewy Riesling. The palate is dense and pleasingly rounded, offering some lime and kerosene notes. Panelists remarked that this is a wine that really needs some time to show its stuff. Buy by the case and drink now through 2008.

Cave Spring Cellars 2000 Off-Dry Riesling
Niagara Peninsula $ (234583)
A beauty. Cave Spring's off-dry model delivers great flavours and a big, racy finish that balances the wine's sweetness. There's nothing cloying or candy-coated about this stylish wine. If anything the fuller flavours make this wine that much more versatile. Think of it as your white for any and every occasion. Open a bottle to sip, quaff with friends or to accompany a good book.

Cilento Wines 2000 Reserve Riesling
Niagara Peninsula $ (605725)
Cilento's 2000 is an elegant, slightly austere Riesling, which displays chalky mineral characters and pleasantly peachy overtones. "A wet cement aroma" was one favourable note, a flight-of-wine-judge-fancy that will likely inspire gales of laughter from casual consumers. Wet cement? Hey, laugh all you want as long as you try this wine. It's funny, but true. It's also extremely tasty.

Hernder Estate Wines 2000 Riesling
Niagara Peninsula $ (332239)
Quietly, determinedly, Hernder Estates has asserted itself as one of the nation's finest Riesling producers as this dry white will happily attest. Classic lime and citrus aromas and bright citrus flavours on the palate are hallmark Niagara Riesling. The wine is lively and beautifully balanced. It's perfect as an aperitif or with light dishes.

Stoney Ridge Cellars 1999 Riesling Reserve
Niagara Peninsula $ (314666)

Stoney Ridge's Reserve is a Niagara Riesling that had panelists singing hits from Men at Work's *Business As Usual* album. Surely this was an Australian ringer, they protested. How else do you explain the huge petrol and warm toast aromas and the big ripe flavours? Thank 1999's warm harvest for this intense, rich Riesling rounded out with a lemony finish. It's drinking wonderfully now, but will continue to age. It's got a long life ahead of it. Enjoy with or without Vegemite sandwiches.

Strewn Wines 1998 Riesling Terroir
Strewn Vineyard
Niagara Peninsula $ (467613)

A rich, densely textured dry wine, with the whiff of lemons and huge citrusy flavours supported by a bright framework of acidity. The winemakers on the panel all sighed, "I wish I had made this wine." An Alsatian model of Riesling, this is a dry white that will age for the next decade. It's massive and supremely structured—the wine equivalent of Barnett Newman's *Voice of Fire* painting. Some look at the painting and see three stripes of colour; others marvel as the piece crackles and hums. This tightly drawn wine isn't for everyone, but there's an audience out there that will marvel as this wine crackles and hums in their glass.

Thirteenth Street Wine Co. 2000
G.H. Funk Vineyards Riesling
Niagara Peninsula $

This is a classic Niagara Riesling, with excellent weight and a soft lemony finish standing out among its many charms. Deep aromas of honey and apricot mingle with some tropical fruit notes. The palate is enhanced by a touch of sweetness and ripe fruit flavours. This is a concentrated and age-worthy wine with a finish that goes on and on. Drink now through 2010.

Vineland Estates Winery 2000
Semi-Dry Riesling
Niagara Peninsula $ (232033)

The off-dry companion to Vineland's *Vines* Award winner, this wine's balance of crisp acidity and richly concentrated fruit floored the panel. Grapefruit and lime aromas, and a delicious core of fruit cut with a quicksilver seam of acidity that refreshes the flavours on the finish. It's a lush wine that will make friends easily. Keep a bottle in the fridge at all times—just in case.

Vineland Estates Winery 1999
Riesling Reserve
Niagara Peninsula $$ (316307)

To paraphrase American pop singer Pink, this wine's coming up so you'd better get the party started. On the nose, this is unmistakably Riesling. Petrol and lemon aromas hover above the glass. Richly textured, showing kerosene and flint accents to the strong citrus flavours. A dry white with good length and high acidity, this is a good candidate for six-plus years in the cellar. Serve well chilled with shellfish or as an aperitif.

RECOMMENDED

Cave Spring Cellars 2000 Reserve Riesling
Niagara Peninsula $ (286377)

The leesy lime notes announce the arrival of a serious-minded Riesling. For some, those funky notes are a signal to move on to the next bottle, but for German Riesling aficionados, it's time to fill that wine glass and start a dialogue with it. There's a delicious core of fruit lurking behind the concentrated earthy, nutty accents. It's lush, with a succulent acidity driving the lingering finish.

Cave Spring Cellars CSV 2000 Riesling
Niagara Peninsula $$ (566026)

This vibrant white features fleshy peach flavours and a rapier-like lemon zest acidity that balances the hint of residual sugar on the palate. This concentrated young wine benefits from some deep leesy and complex mineral notes—it's a bit funky when you first pull the cork. Offering good value for the price, it deserves to be served with stir-fries and salads, or better yet, salmon. Put one away until 2010 and amaze your friends and yourself with the complexity of this powerful white.

CedarCreek Estate Winery 2001 Riesling Dry
Okanagan Valley $ (217166)

A rich and velvety wine that delivers sweet citrus aromas and a fresh, focussed palate reminiscent of ruby red grapefruit and white peach. This wine's broad, rich lemony profile and easy structure will win legions of fans. Drink now through 2006.

Daniel Lenko Estate Winery 2000 Reserve Riesling
Niagara Peninsula $

Lenko offers a young wine that is subtle enough to match with your favourite steamed seafood or grilled white meat, but also well-rounded enough to linger around the table afterwards to gossip and talk politics. A beam of acidity supports the medium-bodied profile and moderate concentration.

Featherstone Estate Winery 2000 Off-Dry Riesling
Niagara Peninsula $

Succulent apricot and peach aromas carry over to the palate of this nicely balanced off-dry Riesling. A pleasant sipping wine, it will help launch a thousand conversations about the news of the world, politics and what it will take for Tom Hanks to win another Oscar.

Hawthorne Mountain Vineyards 2000 Riesling
Okanagan Valley $ (440693)

This ripe, round model of Riesling has lovely mango and tropical fruit flavours and kiwi aromas. A solid sipping wine, it would have scored off the charts if the palate held more richness and concentration. Light and lean, this is a food-friendly wine that screams out for grilled fish served with fruit chutney. Drink now.

Henry of Pelham Family Estate Winery 2000 Reserve Riesling
Niagara Peninsula $ (283291)

Good tropical fruit aromas—especially mango and ripe pineapple—were showered with great praise from our panel. On the palate, there's firm, rich structure and fine balance between the bright acidity and concentrated fruit flavours. Nice wine.

Hillebrand Estates 2001 Trius Riesling Dry
Niagara Peninsula $ (303792)

Brilliant peach and apricot fruit are front-and-centre in this nicely balanced and structured wine. The acidity kicks in mid palate, picking up a hint of bitterness or tartness on the finish. Slim and compact, but in a harmonious way. Drink now.

Inniskillin Wines 2000 Riesling
Niagara Peninsula $ (083790)

Atypical yet delicious. Rich, dry wine with a tight green apple and citrus nose and apple fruit flavours. This wine didn't scream Riesling, which accounts for its three-star finish. But for straight-up enjoyment, this is highly recommended wine. Its crisp palate is offset by vivid structure. Cellar for a year or two for maximum enjoyment. The panel suggests this is a sleeper with plenty of wow potential in its future.

Peller Estates 2000 Private Reserve Dry Riesling

Niagara Peninsula $ (981290)

Peller's dry white would be right at home in a picnic basket. Its delicate peach and floral notes are more in line with a romantic nosh in the shade for two than, say, the annual company barbecue. But an outgoing wine like this is too classy to discriminate, even if there are sack races going on. It's the life of any party.

Quails' Gate Estate Winery 2001 Dry Riesling Limited Release

Okanagan Valley $ (308312)

Clean and focussed, this is a delicious Riesling thanks to abundant apricot and citrus aromas. Still young and backward, it doesn't offer much in the way of aroma now, but the purity and intensity of fruit on the palate promise wondrous things are going to reveal themselves as it ages.

Southbrook Winery 1998 Riesling Lailey Vineyard

Niagara Peninsula $ (448324)

Sweaty petrol aromas point this offbeat Riesling towards the wet dog sector of the wine aroma wheel. On the palate, it's full and rich with complex notes of peach pit emerging on the finish.

Strewn Wines 1998 Riesling Süssreserve

Niagara Peninsula $ (470419)

"Süssreserve" is a winemaking term that indicates the winemaker reintroduced some unfermented grape juice into the wine before bottling. It's a technique that adds some natural sweetness to the wine and can enhance the roundness of the mouth-feel. In this case, panelists enjoyed the sweetish mid palate, but noted a lack of substance. Enjoy as a sipping wine or pair with spicy Chinese or Thai dishes.

Wild Goose Vineyards 2000 Riesling
Okanagan Valley $ (414730)
A charmingly aromatic wine, with pungent floral and Muscat-like grape aromas, this Riesling was highlighted by tasters for its many olfactory graces. Like the perfume counter at Holt Renfrew, it's intoxicating, which makes for an excellent first impression. Unfortunately the palate doesn't live up to the aromas. This sweetly perfumed wine is great for romantic dinners, but be warned it's a bit of a conversation killer. It's hard to whisper sweet nothings when your date's nose is stuck deep inside a wineglass.

QUITE GOOD

Ancient Coast 2000 Riesling
Niagara Peninsula $
Candied fruit and mineral notes add interest to this crisp, clean wine. Its peachy flavours make for an engaging, enjoyable wine, which offers good value for its price.

Domaine Combret 1994 Riesling
Reserve Estate Bottled
Fraser Valley $$ (358515)
Here's an aged Riesling with petrol and toasty lemon characteristics that is more interesting than enjoyable. Any fruit has dropped off—as it does in all Rieslings as they age—leaving behind a huge searing acidity. Serve with food for best enjoyment.

Harbour Estates Winery 2000 Riesling
Niagara Peninsula $
This crisp, clean Riesling makes the most of its peach and grapefruit flavours and long lingering finish. An excellent food wine, it will make fish tacos and spicy black beans sing.

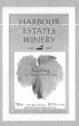

Hernder Estate Wines 2001 Riesling

Niagara Peninsula $ (332239)

Peachy aromas and flavours stand out in this enjoyable wine. The palate is sweet to the point of being candied. Fans of wines boasting a hit of residual sugar take note.

Hernder Estate Wines 2000 Reserve Riesling

Niagara Peninsula $ (554238)

Here's a young reserve with some faint Riesling notes, especially in its meaty, complex nose. The wine is enjoyably round on the palate, but only offers a slight glimpse of varietal character. This is a very reserved reserve.

Inniskillin Wines 2001 Riesling Late Autumn

Niagara Peninsula $ (219543)

More than one taster remarked that this is a four-star wine, but it's not a four-star Riesling. The aromas and flavours are more Sauvignon Blanc than Riesling, which saw its ranking plummet. If you're looking for a classic Riesling you'd be better off looking elsewhere; however, if it's a crisp, vibrant white wine you're after, buy a case of this tangy charmer.

Jackson-Triggs Niagara Estate 2000 Dry Riesling Proprietors' Reserve

Niagara Peninsula $ (526277)

An approachable, if one-dimensional Riesling that makes the most of its intense aromatics: honey, citrus and floral notes. Soft on the palate, with a tart fruit finish.

Jackson-Triggs Niagara Estate 2000 Proprietors' Grand Reserve Riesling

Niagara Peninsula $ (593988)

Jackson-Triggs reserve is a fresh, aromatic Riesling with positive fruit aromas. The fruit returns on the finish. Despite its posh Grand Reserve labelling, this is an extremely versatile wine to serve whenever you fancy. There's nothing formal about it.

Konzelmann Estate Winery 2000 Grand Reserve Classic

Niagara Peninsula $$$$ (605378)

Konzelmann's Grand Reserve Classic is extremely aromatic and very tasty, but it lacks the authority of its exclusive price. On the palate, it is fruity and moderately sweet. Floral aromas and mineral green apple flavours make for a wonderful sipping wine.

Konzelmann Estate Winery 2000 Riesling

Niagara Peninsula $ (200501)

Ripe peach and floral notes, along with a hint of petrol, are the drawing cards of this appealing wine. The petrol returns on the palate of this off-dry Riesling, which is harmonious right through to the delicate kiss of lemon on the finish.

Lailey Vineyard 2000 Riesling

Niagara Peninsula $

This light, delicate Riesling built with the dinner table in mind offers some rich mineral and lime notes. On the palate, it's clean and balanced, but lacks fruit.

Lakeview Cellars 2000 Beamsville Bench Riesling Vinc Vineyard

Niagara Peninsula $ (307157)

This dry Riesling shows power and length. Bracing acidity and a good core of citrus fruit are the hall-marks of this engaging white wine. The finish lingers.

Marynissen Estates 2000 Riesling Marynissen Vineyard

Niagara Peninsula $

Good tropical fruit character and an interesting flinty character on the palate. This is an unassuming, extremely enjoyable wine to enjoy over the next two years.

Mission Hill Family Estate 2001 Riesling Dry

Okanagan Valley $ (220848)

A wine with excellent weight and balance, it needs time for the flavours and aromas to open up. The structure impressed the panelists, who predicted the signs of a great wine emerging in the coming year.

Reif Estate Winery 2001 Riesling Estate Bottled

Niagara Peninsula $ (111799)

Wet wool, wet dog and mineral notes are featured in this Germanic-style Niagara Riesling. Don't let those descriptors throw you—good palate weight and intensity make for a rich, rewarding wine to enjoy by the glass or with a meal.

Stoney Ridge Cellars 1999 Riesling Bench

Niagara Peninsula $ (287334)

Rich citrus notes peek out from behind the strong kerosene aromas and flavours in this rich, enjoyable Riesling. The petrol flavours that linger on the palate are one of Riesling's acquired tastes.

Strewn Wines 1994 Riesling

Niagara Peninsula $

Canned peach and a bright acidity are the dominant character of this mature Riesling. The zesty acid has preserved this wine, keeping it fresh and vibrant in the bottle. Try this and see what you think about aged Riesling.

Thirty Bench Wines 2000 Riesling

Niagara Peninsula $

Fresh fruit flavours and a lively snap of acidity make this a nice accompaniment to grilled fish and poultry with creamy sauces or a modest cheese plate. This wine also has enough fat and fruit to be enjoyed by itself as an aperitif.

Thirty Bench Wines 1999 Riesling Dry

Niagara Peninsula $

A big Riesling nose of petrol and citrus pave the way for this wine's full-bodied texture. It's intense and rich, but lacks fruit and finishes with a tart bitterness. Best enjoyed with a meal.

Thirty Bench Wines 1999 Riesling Limited Yield Semi-Dry

Niagara Peninsula $$

Peaches and a honeyed sweetness stand out on the palate of this lush, slightly oily textured wine. Drink now.

Thomas and Vaughan Vintners 2001 Off-Dry Riesling

Niagara Peninsula $

Peach aromas and ripe peach flavours present themselves, mingled with some citrus and dusty nutty notes, in this pleasantly quaffable wine. Flavourful and concentrated, this is a crowd-pleasing sipper.

Wild Goose Vineyards 2001 Riesling Dry Reserve

Okanagan Valley $ (434316)

Here's a wine that could be dubbed Memories of a Peach Canning Factory. Sweet peaches dominate the aromas and flavours of this honeyed wine. The sweet hit is a little over the top and throws the wine out of balance.

SAUVIGNON BLANC

Wines produced from Sauvignon Blanc offer freshness, flavour and real concentration of fruit that is
best enjoyed young. The classic white's characteristic aggressive zestiness is one of its charms.
Age dulls that most recognizably Sauvignon Blanc
note and, in turn, dulls the enjoyment of the wine.
Call this the wine world's equivalent to a one-hit
wonder—a glorious burst of fame, then nothing
but a fleeting residual vapour trail.

Other classic varietal characteristics include
gooseberries, cut grass or other herbaceous
notes such as asparagus and green peppers, figs,
green apples and grapefruit—and cat pee (yes,
cat pee; don't wince). Archetypal French Sauvignon
Blanc from Sancerre and Pouilly-Fumé can offer a
whiff of, how do you say, *pipi de chat*. You might,
however, be happy to hear that there's little tomcat
stench in most fruit-forward New World examples,
including Ontario and B.C. bottles, but they lack

FOOD PAIRING SUGGESTIONS
Oysters and scallops,
goat cheese or brie and
other semi-soft cheeses,
white fish such as picker-
el or halibut, pasta with
pesto or cream sauces.
Sauvignon Blanc is also
extremely vegetarian
friendly. It's a zesty partner for vegetable risotto,
mixed salads, vegetable
skewers or stir-fries.

the aging potential of their elegant French cousins. In extremely ripe Sauvignon, the fruit notes become more tropical in nature. Papaya and passion fruit are common descriptors.

Sauvignon has been grown for centuries in France. The rest of the wine world has only caught on in the past two decades or so. New Zealand has led the charge, producing some of the more impressive Sauvignon Blancs in the world. South Africa is running right behind. Sauvignon Blancs from New World wine regions are gaining popularity with consumers because of their upfront and attractive fruit characteristics. A growing number of dedicated vintners in British Columbia and Ontario are falling in step with their counterparts in New Zealand, South Africa, California and Australia.

The success of Sauvignon Blanc in Ontario and British Columbia seems assured if the wines are simply made. Oak-aged wines, which are some-times, though frustratingly not always, identified on the label or are called Fumé Blanc, risk losing the bright, fresh fruit flavour, but just as the lesson of subtle oak aging was learned with Chardonnay, so too will domestic vintners tame the two-by-four thwack of their Sauvignons.

Sumac Ridge winemaker Mark Wendenburg produces a non-oaked, private reserve Sauvignon Blanc each year, and uses the grape as the main component for a blended white wine. From his vantage, the keys to lively and flavourful Sauvignon are choosing an ideal site and harvesting ripe fruit. He added that his job is aided greatly by the Okanagan's natural climate—the cool nights and warm days help preserve fruit flavours and acidity in the grapes. "I personally am not looking for inspiration from New Zealand or France but rather to develop our own style and flavours unique to the Okanagan," he said.

While the *Vines* panel didn't confer the coveted *Vines* Award in the Sauvignon Blanc category, the tasting proved to be eye opening. The majority of submissions were rated three stars or higher, which speaks to the overall quality of Canadian Sauvignon Blanc.

Tasting Panel: RD, SGB, WS, CW

HIGHLY RECOMMENDED

Cilento Wines 2001 Sauvignon Blanc Reserve
Niagara Peninsula $$ (510251)
This has all the markings of a great Sauvignon Blanc. Fresh asparagus, peach and gooseberry create a sensational and intense aroma, with gooseberry, peach and lemon grass notes dominating the palate. This is a big, round wine—it's truly heavy duty. A nice balance of acidity gives the finish an added edge. Excellent with freshwater fish such as pickerel, trout and perch.

Creekside Estate Winery 2001 Sauvignon Blanc
Niagara Peninsula $$ (572206)
This is a very attractive wine. The aromas are a successful combination of pear, honey and gooseberry, announcing the arrival of a serious sipper. With its zingy, zesty style, this is nice crisp wine with citrus flavours and a pleasing streak of acidity that carries through to the finish.

Mission Hill Cordillera 2001 Spotted Lake Sauvignon Blanc
Okanagan Valley $ (596007)
This elegant, easy-drinking wine offers typical grassy herbal aromas and ripe fruit capped by a refreshing lime zest note. An excellent wine to buy by the case for all of your warm-weather entertaining needs, from picnics to impromptu mid week barbecues, or as a good antidote to a hot summer night. It's a nice wine to sip or enjoy with brunch, or with white meat or fish served with a fruit salsa or chutney.

Peller Estates Private Reserve 2000 Sauvignon Blanc Barrel Aged

Niagara Peninsula $ (981308)

Traditional gooseberry and grassy aromas stand out in this benchmark Niagara Sauvignon Blanc. The fresh mouth-feel and refreshing acidity make this a fabulous food wine, perfect to kick off an elegant dinner party. It is flavourful enough to serve to guests as they arrive and can carry them through the appetizer course. Drink now.

Peninsula Ridge Estates Winery 2001 Sauvignon Blanc

Niagara Peninsula $$ (592303)

The follow-up vintage to the 2000 *Vines* Award winner, Peninsula Ridge's new Sauvignon Blanc is another aromatic charmer, with pungent grassy herbal aromas. Gooseberry and green apple flavours come through on the palate, along with a bright acidity and slight sweetness on the finish. This is a wine with solid character and terrific intensity that is best enjoyed in the coming year.

RECOMMENDED

Château des Charmes Winery 2000 Sauvignon Blanc St. Davids Bench Vineyard

Niagara Penisula $ (391300)

Sweet aromas of honey, peach and pineapple stand out. On the palate, there's a bounty of sweet fruit flavours that carry through the lingering finish. Don't let the sugary descriptors fool you, this is a dry wine best enjoyed with food.

Henry of Pelham Family Estate Winery 2001 Sauvignon Blanc

Niagara Peninsula $ (430546)

Nice grassy aromas with pear, apple and gooseberry notes. Pear and honey flavours dance across the palate, offering a fine balance between tart acidity and sweetness. Try with a fresh green salad, goat cheese and chicken pâté.

Hillebrand Estates 2001 Vineyards Series Sauvignon Blanc

Niagara Peninsula $ (386128)

Aromas of green pepper and grass announce the arrival of a decidedly herbal model of Sauvignon Blanc. This is fat and flavourful, with a good roundness and a gust of gooseberry fruit that rustles through the thick grassy notes. Drink now.

Marynissen Estates 2001 Sauvignon Blanc

Niagara Peninsula $

Slightly smoky nose and lemony fruit on the palate make for a rich wine with a sweet burst of flavour. This is an excellent sipping wine, with a balancing tart acidity and a long, lingering finish.

Mission Hill Family Estate Winery 2000 Sauvignon Blanc Reserve

Okanagan Valley $$ (590349)

Aromas of gooseberry and grass and a lively finish are the hallmarks of this straightforward white that's rich, round and extremely enjoyable by the glass. A full-bodied wine, it is a clean, crisp white that's extremely crowd-pleasing. Serve with lighter pastas and dishes that use a squeeze of lemon.

Sandhill 2001 Sauvignon Blanc Burrowing Owl Vineyard

Okanagan Valley $ (587048)

Pink grapefruit and ripe tropical fruit aromas and flavours add some excitement to this bright, focussed Sauvignon Blanc. The fruit flavours are developed and linger on the palate, with a tart bitterness that kept this wine from scoring even higher with the panel.

Strewn Wines 2000 Sauvignon Blanc

Niagara Peninsula $ (582544)

The tasters had this oak-aged wine pegged as a Chardonnay, thanks to its buttery, creamy texture and soft acidity. Oak and vanilla aromas dominate and make for an unusual but enjoyable wine.

Sumac Ridge Estate Winery 2001 Private Reserve Sauvignon Blanc

Okanagan Valley $$ (593087)

Smoky oak aromas and delicate fruit notes combine in this pleasingly complex nose. Oak flavours and tart acidity dominate on the palate. This is a vegetarian-friendly wine that would pair nicely with stir-fries or grilled vegetable skewers.

Sumac Ridge Estate Winery 2001 Sauvignon Blanc

Okanagan Valley $ (731737)

Great varietal character, with grassy, herbal and gooseberry notes present and accounted for. On the palate, the tropical fruit flavours sing for a supper of pasta with pesto and/or salmon and asparagus.

Vineland Estates Winery 2000 Sauvignon Blanc

Niagara Peninsula $ (563361)

All the classic aromas clamour for attention: gooseberry, grapefruit, minerals and grass, with mint and honey notes adding to the commotion. On the palate, there's citrus and sweet tropical fruit. Great mouth-feel and a long finish.

QUITE GOOD

Colio Estate Vineyards 1999 CEV Sauvignon Blanc Barrel-Aged

Lake Erie North Shore $ (500462)

Judicious oak aging has added some spice and creaminess to this full-flavoured wine. A big-boned Blanc, it screams out for roasted chicken, smoked haddock, steamed mussels or dishes with chèvre, brie or feta cheeses.

Lailey Vineyard 2000 Sauvignon Blanc

Niagara Peninsula $$

Here's a leaner, harder-edged Sauvignon Blanc
with elderflower and grassy aromas and flavours.
Pair with an omelet with fresh goat cheese, onion
and asparagus or grilled red and yellow peppers
on focaccia.

OTHER WHITE WINES

Other Whites

If everyone were the same, the world would be a pretty boring place. The same goes for wine. A number of wineries and grape growers in British Columbia and Ontario are experimenting with non-traditional varietals. They plant small acres of little-known vinifera vines such as Viognier, Muscat, Chenin Blanc and others to see what the result will be in both quality and quantity. Sometimes the results are amazing, sometimes forgettable, yet if it weren't for experimentation, Canada wouldn't be producing quality vinifera table wines, or even Icewine.

In fact, most of Canada's early wine production came from experimenting with hybrid grapes. Hybrid grapes result from the crossing of two varietals in hopes of making a new grape that is adaptable to its surrounding environment. Due to

the cool climate of Canada's wine regions, there have been many experiments that have produced interesting wines over the years. The best-known white hybrid in Canada is the Vidal grape; its hardiness and thick skin make it an ideal late harvest and Icewine grape.

So, we feel it's our duty to review the odd white wines—the ones that you may not see on liquor store shelves. This way, if you happen to stumble upon one on a wine tour, you can be the cool kid in the yard, setting the trend for others to follow.

Tasting Panel: PB, TK, GP, WS, CW

HIGHLY RECOMMENDED

Château des Charmes Winery 2000 Estate Auxerrois

Niagara Peninsula $ (114058)

Auxerrois is used by the French primarily as a blending grape. Not known to be overly aromatic or flavourful, its best feature tends to be its levels of acidity, which give the wine added depth. In Canada, only a few select wineries produce the wine. This Château des Charmes 2000 offering is the best example of a well-made Auxerrois. A light peach and pink grapefruit nose gives way to a bright, crisp mouth-feel that lifts the fruit ever so slightly. If you're in the mood for sushi or oysters, this would be an ideal wine to enhance the food, but not overpower it. Great value.

Jackson-Triggs Okanagan Estate 2000 Proprietors' Reserve Viognier

Okanagan Valley $ (593129)

Most benchmark Viogniers hail from the northern Rhône, where the grape is able to fully ripen yet maintain the important acid levels that make for a full-bodied, aromatic and crisp white. In Canada, only a few vintners produce Viognier but J-T

appears to be leading the charge as more wineries are producing it every year. This 2000 Viognier is a good example of the important balance between acidity and ripeness. It has a wonderful aroma of anise, grapefruit and hints of apricot and peach. The expressive fruit led by apricot, kiwi and peach is enhanced with a nice line of crisp acidity. Best enjoyed with pork roast, grilled chicken breast or steamed veggies over a bed of wild rice.

Quails' Gate Estate Winery 2000 Chenin Blanc Limited Release
Okanagan Valley $ (391854)
Chenin Blanc is a lesser-known white that has done wonderfully well in France and South Africa. Quails' Gate has managed to capture the essence of this grape in its 2000 offering. Known for its higher-than-normal acidity and resulting tart taste, it's a hard wine to nail. This Chenin Blanc opens with a gorgeous fragrance of fresh kiwi, passion fruit and a hint of banana. On the palate, the wine simply explodes with melon, grapefruit and green apple. The acids lift the fruit all the way through to the finish. Balanced and crisp, this wine sparkles. Get what you can before it's all gone and enjoy with sea fare such as crab legs, shrimp and mussels or with a pork-based dish.

RECOMMENDED

Calona Vineyards 2000 Sovereign Opal
Okanagan Valley $ (364265)
Described as a brashy wine, this has a lot of fruit fighting for independence. Intense aromas of lemon, lime and swatches of floral perfume. The palate is dominated by lemon and kiwi flavours with an interesting oily mouth-feel. A light white that is refreshing when chilled and flavourful enough to serve as a cocktail before dinner.

Château des Charmes Winery 2000 Estate Aligoté

Niagara Peninsula $ (284950)

Aligoté is widely recognized as the poor cousin of Chardonnay. Produced primarily in Burgundy, the little grape that really can't has found a home at Château des Charmes. This 2000 offering manages to extract a lot from a little, considering Aligoté is known for its higher acid levels and low body weight. Delicate notes of grapefruit open up to a racy acidity that gives a heftiness to the wine. Definitely built for food, this wine has enough acidity to cut through spicy Asian or Indian dishes.

Château des Charmes Winery 2000 Viognier St. Davids Bench Vineyard

Niagara Peninsula $ (432948)

A charming Viognier with lush notes of banana, grapefruit and peach. The transfer of fruit to the palate is not as upfront as you would expect from the intense aromas. Streaks of tropical fruit dash in between the lines of acidity. A slightly hot finish with an interesting oily texture rounds out this well-made white. Great match for lightly seasoned fish and white meats but ensure your seasonings are not too intense, as this wine has a delicate nature.

Featherstone Estate Winery 2000 Vidal Blanc

Ontario $

One of the first offerings from a newly minted winery in Niagara, Featherstone's 2000 Vidal is a fine example of how to handle this hybrid grape. Normally built with a lot of upfront tropical candied fruit, this Vidal has instead been dipped in oak to mellow down the fruit. Light notes of pear, pineapple and a touch of vanilla make an appealing introduction. Flavourful tropical fruits are balanced by a toasty coating on the palate. An added layer of acidity provides this white with enough weight to carry both the fruit and oak through to the finish. This would be a fine alternative to oaked Chardonnay.

Peller Estates 2000 Vineyard Series Muscat
Niagara Peninsula $ (981373)

An intensely perfumed grape varietal, Muscat is not a widely produced wine. Sought by some white-wine nuts for its relatively obscure production levels, Peller's 2000 offering captures the beauty of a well-made Muscat wine. Huge notes of lychee nut and peach with a perfumed splash of rosewater make for an attractive fragrance. Sweet candied peach and pineapple flavours are lightly lifted by a soft acidity. If you're looking for a white to entertain the masses, this Muscat will not disappoint.

Reif Estate Winery 2001 Trollinger X Riesling Estate
Niagara Peninsula $ (201236)

No, it's not named after Malcolm X. The "X" stands for cross, referring to the two grape varietals that were grafted together to produce an offspring. Also called Kerner, this one is more like a Sauvignon Blanc with strong notes of cat pee, lemon and tangerine. There's a thin layer of sweetness on the palate with lemon and pineapple flavours. A nice crisp acidity and slightly tart finish. Best enjoyed chilled with oysters and tiger shrimp cocktails.

Thomas and Vaughan Vintners 2001 Vidal Semi-Sweet
Ontario $

A typical Niagara Vidal with lush lemon, pear and green apple characteristics. The fruit explodes on the palate with a touch of sweetness up front. More citrus flavours follow through to the finish. Nice undertones of pineapple round out a well-made wine. Best enjoyed lounging around on a Sunday afternoon.

QUITE GOOD

Ancient Coast 2000 Vidal
Ontario $ (559070)

A consumer-friendly Vidal with typical tropical notes of pear and pineapple. A touch of sweetness adds to the fruity flavours. A good value wine that would be ideal for larger social gatherings.

Château des Charmes Winery 1998 Savagin St. Davids Bench Vineyard
Niagara Peninsula $ (432955)

If you're looking for an obscure wine, this is one you should search out—if only to say you've tasted a Savagin. Produced mainly in France, Savagin is a late-ripening grape, which makes it even more odd for a Niagara winery to produce. Lychee aromas with a hint of nuttiness. More nutty and floral on the palate with a short, but clean finish. Although showing signs of aging, there's some life left to showcase this one-of-a-kind white.

Cilento Wines 2000 Renaissance Seyval Blanc
Ontario $

A French hybrid widely planted in Niagara in the 1980s, Seyval Blanc has all but disappeared from the vineyards. Yet, Cilento has managed to produce one that is both appealing and very affordable. A mix of pine nut and lemon aromas gives way to pineapple, lemon and grapefruit flavours. A lack of acidity makes for a light, short finish. This would be an ideal wine for the large wedding where wine is not a priority, but needs to be on the table.

Hillebrand Estates 2001 Muscat Reserve Vineyard Select

Niagara Peninsula $ (291518)

Not as intensely fragrant as Muscat can be, this lightly perfumed white has honey and lychee characters. Leaning towards Gewürztraminer in style and flavours, there's a sweet hit on the palate with fine lines of acidity that carry the fruit to a short finish. This would be a good match for those who like Thai dishes with only a mild level of hot spice.

Hillside Estate 2001 Kerner

Okanagan Valley $ (505180)

This popular German grape is another recent addition to the world of wine. Introduced by Germany in the late 1960s, it's a cross between the red grape Trollinger and Riesling. Built for cooler climates, Kerner is produced by a couple of wineries in Canada. Hillside's Kerner has Del Monte tropical fruit characteristics. The candied fruit carries over to the palate. The light acidity leaves the fruit waning through the finish. Search out if only to try a niche wine.

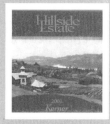

Hillside Estate 2001 Muscat Ottonel

Okanagan Valley $$ (434803)

Muscat Ottonel is a relative newcomer in the world of grapes. A lighter version of Muscat, Hillside's 2001 offering has subtle citrus notes. On the palate, the wine is given a lift with some acidity, but it can't seem to carry through to the finish, which is common in most Muscat Ottonels. This one needs food—sushi, oysters and other raw seafood with light seasoning would be a good match.

House of Rose Winery 1998 Sémillon—The Green Rose
Okanagan Valley $ (537050)

Sémillon is a widely planted grape that lacks the profile and prestige of Sauvignon Blanc or Riesling. Although not produced by many Canadian wineries, it has shown success in Washington State and New Zealand. House of Rose has taken this cooler-climate grape under its care. Although the results are mixed, this 1998 Sémillon is showing signs of its age. Exotic spice (think ginger) and lemon bounce off each other from start to finish. With the acids starting to level out, this is a great match for spicy Thai, but not for much longer.

Lailey Vineyard 2000 Vidal
Ontario $

Made in a dry style, this Vidal had one panelist reminiscing about his love of freshly cut rhubarb. Notes of lemon and pineapple round out the aromas. The rhubarb profile continues on the palate with subtle flavours of peach blossom and pineapple. It's a clean, crisp white great for those with a low threshold for acidity.

Pillitteri Estates Winery 2000 Vidal Semi-Dry
Ontario $ (349100)

Honeyed lemon with a hint of beeswax gives way to more lemon and grapefruit on the palate. A lack of acidity prevents the fruit from really exploding on the palate, but an oily texture gives this Vidal a different feel.

St. Hubertus Estate Winery 2000 Bacchus
Okanagan Valley $ (344994)

A cross between Riesling and Müller-Thurgau, the hybrid comes off as a member of the Sauvignon Blanc family. This Bacchus is more subdued in its personality. Lemon and lime with a toasty note give way to a crisp, yet lean-on-the-fruit-side wine. Lack of depth prevents a food pairing, but it

would be an enjoyable summer sipper. This is the last vintage for this wine at St. Hubertus.

White Blends

Why blend white wine? With the majority of New World wine consumers focussed on single varietal wines, it would seem to be fruitless to blend off two whites and risk confusing the wine consumer even more. Yet, in Canada there's a handful of producers who buck the trend by releasing white concoctions that are all over the wine map. Most of the white blends in this section are light on the wallet, with the exception of Sumac Ridge's White Meritage, and they shouldn't be taken too seriously. Most wineries that produce mixed whites are generally creating easy-to-drink, no-thinking-required wines. Chill out and enjoy.
Tasting Panel: TP, WS, CW, AW

HIGHLY RECOMMENDED

Sumac Ridge Estate Winery 2000 Meritage (White)

Okanagan Valley $$ (434977)
Sumac Ridge was the first winery in Canada to apply the American-coined term to its premium Bordeaux-style blends, including the white counterpart of the more popular red Meritage. Although a number of wineries now refer to their premium red blends as "Meritage," Sumac is one of the only wineries to slap the term on its white premium wine. The 2000 Meritage is constructed from a blend of Sauvignon Blanc and Semillon grapes. Having spent some time in barrels, it has distinctive notes of toasty Cheerios with ginger and lemon. On the palate, there's a weighty feeling created by the oak and high acidity. Herbaceous flavours from the Sauvignon Blanc dominate with hints of lemon. Capped by a lengthy spicy finish, this is a wonderfully complex

wine that could stand tall on any table that features smoked salmon, grilled pork and pasta with cream sauce.

Wild Goose Vineyards 2001 Autumn Gold
Okanagan Valley $ (414755)
A consistently well-made wine that captures the essence of white blends. Unlike red blends constructed to last in the cellar, most white blends in this category are built for early consumption. Autumn Gold is a tasty treat that has no pretensions of needing time in the cellar. This one is all about the fruit. Tantalizing aromas of peach, pear and pineapple give way to an off-dry white full of flavours. The ripe fruit flavours are heightened by a racy acidity that is balanced by its residual sugar. Great wine to chill down and enjoy on the patio or on your next picnic.

RECOMMENDED

Birchwood Estate Wines 2000 Gewürztraminer Riesling
Niagara Peninsula $ (572156)
A Gewürztraminer-heavy blend that captures the spicy lychee characters of a G-wine with subtle tones of citrus from the Riesling. Bright acidity with a touch of residual sugar balances the flavours of candied fruit of lychee, nutmeg and lemon. It is an enjoyable blend best suited to spicy hot dishes or hot chicken wings.

Cave Spring Cellars 2000 Auxerrois-Pinot Blanc
Niagara Peninsula $ (500975)
A simple, crisp white blend that comes across as an Auxerrois with a dash of Pinot Blanc. It has light notes of apple, pear and lemon. On the palate, there's balanced acidity with more intense flavours of grapefruit, peach and apple. A great starter wine to go with a salad.

Inniskillin Wines 2000 Travigne (White)
Niagara Peninsula $ (550962)

Sunshine in a glass. This blend comes across like a Sauvignon Blanc. Lots of freshly mowed grass with a dash of squeezed lemon. Crisp with a nicely balanced acidity that heightens the fresh fruit flavours on the palate. A wine built for simple enjoyment. Pair with casual times at the cottage or on the deck.

Mission Hill Cordillera Okanagan 2001 Wild Horse Canyon
Okanagan Valley $ (574129)

A bushel basket full of fruity goodness. Leaning on the Vidal side with a supporting cast of many different whites, this is a dense wine that has attractive notes of ginger spice with pineapple, peach and lemon. It's thick and viscous on the palate, with robust flavours carried through to the finish with a streak of acidity. Although it falls short on the finish, this is an enjoyable wine designed for front-porch sipping.

Quails' Gate Estate Winery 2001 Chasselas-Pinot Blanc
Okanagan Valley $ (585737)

This blend is primarily composed of the Swiss native grape Chasselas with a touch of Pinot Blanc. The Chasselas grape provides a racy acidity with intense lemon flavours. The dash of Pinot Blanc gives the wine depth and weight with added characters of pear and apple. A good blend that doesn't try too hard, but gives enough to make it enjoyable. As well as being a good conversation sipper, it could handle cream-sauce pasta dishes.

Strewn Wines 1999 Two Vines Riesling Gewürztraminer
Niagara Peninsula $ (467662)

This white shows off its Riesling side with petrol notes and hints of beeswax and lemon. Lighter in style, it has developed an oily texture with floral and petrol flavours. Leaning towards the off-dry style, this wine is complex enough to handle spicy fish dishes and Thai foods. No need to age any longer.

Thirty Bench Wines 2000 Mountainview White
Ontario $

A fifty/fifty blend of Riesling and Vidal combining the racy acidity found in well-made Rieslings with the lush fruit flavours of a Vidal. Dominant pink grapefruit notes with hints of peach and green apple carry over the palate. Bright, crisp and tasty sums up this split-identity blend.

Thornhaven Estates 2000 Sauvignon Blanc–Chardonnay
Okanagan Valley $ (730432)

This Sauvignon Blanc-heavy blend is simply delicious. Crisp, clean flavours of grassy lemon with undertones of peach and apricot. A touch of residual sugar up front with a racy acidity carrying the flavours through to the finish. Pair with appetizers such as sushi, spring rolls and other lightly seasoned offerings.

QUITE GOOD

Featherstone Estate Winery 2000 Gemstone White
Ontario $

A blend of Seyval Blanc and Vidal, this off-dry white has a perfumed blend of peach and soapy lemon. Candied citrus flavours with a slightly oily presence make for an oddly attractive taste. Lush and tasty, this is a simple wine for simple times.

Mission Hill 49 N 1999 Chardonnay, Pinot Blanc, Semillon

Okanagan Valley $ (532853)

Designed to be enjoyed now, this consumer-friendly dry white gives off notes of pear, grapefruit and lemon with a touch of buttery toast. Having spent time in the barrel, it has some depth beyond the fruit, making it a versatile wine for mid week quickie dishes.

Pillitteri Estates Winery 2000 Gewürztraminer Riesling

Niagara Peninsula $ (349126)

Peaches, peaches and more peaches. Although there are hints of ginger spice through this wine, it's a peachy delight. A light acidity leaves the wine a little airy, but the residual sugar gives it an off-dry touch. Simply chill and serve.

Sparkling Wines

A lot of sparkling wines are made in Canada, including enormous vats of Baby Duck and other crackling pop wines made in bulk in giant wine factories. The presence of these so-called sparklers makes it difficult for producers of serious fizz to catch a break. But some estate wineries are staring down the stigma of Moody Blue and Baby Duck, which are more wine cooler than anything else, with exceptional sparklers that are as elegant and fun as the finest Champagne. For the record, only the French region of Champagne makes Champagne, everyone else makes sparkling wine.

Fundamental to the success of all good sparkling wines is a crisp, firm backbone of acidity, which can only be achieved in relatively cool climates. This makes Canada's cool-climate wine regions a natural choice for sparkling wine production. Vintners are using Riesling, Chardonnay, Pinot Noir and Pinot Meunier to produce stylish

FOOD PAIRING SUGGESTIONS
Who needs food? Sparkling wines are fine on their own to celebrate any occasion. After driving for hours to the family cottage in grid-locked traffic, uncork a sparkling wine to wash away all the stress and set the stage for a relaxing weekend.

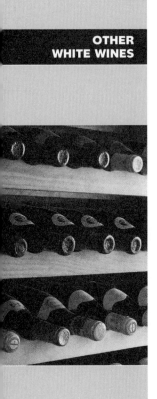

and flavourful wines. Two winemaking methods are generally employed. The Charmat process, or *méthode cuvé close*, sees the wine undergo secondary fermentation in a reinforced stainless steel tank. The more rarefied *méthode traditionelle* has the second fermentation take place in the bottle in which the wine is sold. This is the quality method, which produces tiny pearl string bubbles in the wine. This labour-intensive process means only small lots are produced each year. Some of the wines reviewed might be difficult for consumers to find because they sell out quickly, reappearing only with the next vintage.
Tasting Panel: TP, WS, CW, AW

HIGHLY RECOMMENDED

Henry of Pelham Family Estate Winery 1999 Cuvée Catharine Brut
Niagara Peninsula $$ (616441)
The debut vintage of sparkling wine from Henry of Pelham is an impressive first effort. Made in the classic Champagne style, *méthode traditionelle*, which requires hand riddling, bottle fermentation and a few years of TLC. It has typical notes of yeast, pineapple and peach. Soft and supple on the palate with fine pearl bubbles. Lively yet balanced, this is the perfect wine to match any special Kodak moments.

Thirteenth Street Wine Co. 1998 G.H. Funk Vineyards Premier Cuvée
Niagara Peninsula $$
This is a fabulously frothing fizz. Intense notes of caramel, toffee, yeast and biscuit. Lush mouthfeel with bread cake, more caramel and pineapple flavours. There's also a hint of strawberry from the Pinot Noir side of this classic sparkling wine. Tight pearls with a creamy texture cap off a glorious effort. Pop this cork with good friends.

RECOMMENDED

Cilento Wines Riesling Brut Méthode Cuvé Close

Niagara Peninsula $

This non-vintage has very attractive notes of lavender, pear and honeysuckle. On the palate, there's an interesting oily layer that coats the fruit and balances out the acidity. A grapefruit rind finish caps off a good sparkling that is very reasonably priced.

Hillebrand Estates Trius Brut NV

Niagara Peninsula $$ (451641)

Made in the classic Champagne style, this non-vintage from Hillebrand has typical yeasty notes with a core of peach and apple fruit. Balanced acidity with lively pearls creates a nice mouth-feel that's both soft and racy. A slight mouth-puckering finish places this wine in the cocktail part of the evening served with spicy dips.

Peller Estates Founder's Series Cristalle

Niagara Peninsula $$ (542142)

A truly unique Canadian bent on sparkling wine. Made in the *traditionelle* style, the dosage, which is a small amount of sugar or older wine that is added after the yeast sediment has been removed, is a dash of Icewine. Generous notes of apple, pear and apricot give way to a touch of sweet fruit on the palate. It's like a late harvest with fizz. Great wine for casual gatherings—serve after dinner with a bowl of fresh fruit.

Sumac Ridge Estate Winery 1998 Steller's Jay Brut Méthode Classique
Okanagan Valley $$ (264879)
A rose-tinted sparkling accenting a good percentage of Pinot Noir in the blend. Attractive strawberry, peach and toasty notes. Delicious fruity flavours with strawberry, apple and biscuit characters. A slightly high acidity creates a racy texture with a full-bodied mouth-feel.

Vineland Estates Winery 1999 Riesling Méthode Cuvé Close
Niagara Peninsula $$
Although not as complex as a classically made sparkling wine, this one has notes of lanolin and flinty petrol with lemon. Crisp lemon flavours are accentuated by a racy acidity. Best paired with spicy hors d'oeuvres.

QUITE GOOD

Grape Tree Estate Wines 2000 Hexagon
Lake Erie North Shore $$
Made in the *méthode cuvé close* style, this wine has an added twist. Taking its name from a hexagon, it has six grapes in its composition. It has a mix of flavours, from herbaceous to floral, with a hint of spice. Hot on the finish, it's an interesting take on sparkling wine.

Hawthorne Mountain Vineyards 1996 Chardonnay Blanc de Blancs
Okanagan Valley $$ (536292)
Showing signs of its age, this wine has typical yeasty notes, but there's also an apple core characteristic. Think hot cross buns. Dry in style with tight pearls, it still has a fair amount of acidity. A hot finish knocks the fruit around a bit. No need to age this sparkler any longer—it's ready for your next strawberries-and-cream brunch.

Hawthorne Mountain Vineyards HMV Brut NV Dosage Zero

Okanagan Valley $$ (449702)

In the search for classic Champagne styles, this one gets full marks for technical merits. Ripe apple core, cake bread and lemon aromas give way to tasty strawberry and applesauce flavours. There's a good level of acidity to lift up the wine, but it's made to be very dry. The dryness really hinders its overall appeal. This is definitely a wine that needs some food to soften its rough edges.

Jackson-Triggs Niagara Estate 2000 Proprietors' Reserve

Niagara Peninsula $ (563213)

Easily the most aromatic wine in the tasting. Big peach blossom, lemon and pineapple notes that follow through on the palate. In terms of technical merits, it's clean, crisp and refreshing. Lots of fruit with a good layer of acidity. If you're looking for an affordable opening cocktail wine for a wedding or large social gathering, this would be it.

Pillitteri Estates Winery Spumante Classico

Niagara Peninsula $

Made in the Italian Moscato d'Asti style, this is a fruity sparkler. Comes across like ginger ale with a twist. Light and airy on the palate with a bushel full of ripe candied fruit. A good chilled-down family picnic wine.

PINK WINE

ROSÉ

Summer is a season made for loafing, flaked out in a Muskoka chair with a collection of newspapers, magazines and paperbacks sprawled underfoot, with hints of chlorine, retro tunes and barbecue in the air. Now is not the time for uncorking a prized bottle of Montrachet, Margaux or Mosel. You want a wine that matches the occasion—a burst of sweetness and light.

Like Panama hats, convertibles and that special anxiety about losing weight before going to the beach, rosé wine is an integral part of summer. And the days of drinking sweet, cheaply made rosé in the shade are fading as winemakers craft complex, elegant versions of this refreshing wine.

There are rosés for quaffing on the patio, rosés for sipping between bites of cherry tomato and seared steak and tuna, and rosés that range in colour from pale salmon to shocking pink.

FOOD PAIRING SUGGESTIONS
The range in rosé styles from crisp to sweet means not all rosés can be paired well with food. For a rule of thumb, if the rosé is labelled as "dry," "crisp" or "slightly sweet," it could be paired with grilled white meats such as chicken and pork or with fish. If the rosé leans towards the sweet side in style, it would best be enjoyed on its own or with a fruit dish—think strawberries and cream. Rosés are ideal for summer entertaining of all kinds.

According to taster Linda Bramble, they are "the jewel wines," each with its own charms to be savoured drop by drop.

The opaque, pale colour is key to the enjoyment of rosés, which are continuing to gain popularity in Canada. Their hue and flavour depend largely on the production method and grape varieties used. One style blends finished red wine with finished white (as in the case of our *Vines* Award winner). The resulting colour is pink and the flavours are a blend of complementary characteristics. The more popular style comes from using dark-skinned grapes and limiting the amount of skin contact. The less time fermenting on the skins, the lighter the colour of the finished wine.

The result of both processes is a dry or off-dry wine refreshing enough to be enjoyed on the stickiest August day, but with the appealing red fruit characteristics found in red wines. Each year when we draw up the *Vines* editorial calendar for the coming year, our rosé tasting is always slotted into the summer issue, just as our panel evaluation of sparkling wine and Champagne is earmarked for the holiday book. One year, we ought to switch them. Sparkling wine is great anytime, and a nice, dry rosé is one of the best wines to serve at Thanksgiving and Christmas, two of the toughest meals to match with complementary wines. The colour also adds a blush of romance to the proceedings, which is always welcome.

In seasons past, rosés have gotten the sommelier short shrift as big-spending oenophiles dismissed pink wines as overly sweet and cheap. These rosés shatter the stereotypes.

Tasting Panel: LB, TK, KR, WS, CW

VINES AWARD

Cilento Wines 2001 Renaissance Classic Rosé Riesling
Niagara Peninsula $

The crisp, evocative waves of citrus, lemon and peach flavours had the panel thinking Riesling from the first sip. Cilento has used the noble white grape as the foundation for this intense and very tasty rosé. The characteristic Riesling notes are enhanced by a wash of sweet raspberry flavouring—it's an outstanding blend. Flavourful enough to enjoy by the glass on the deck as guests engage in a game of *Six Degrees of Separation*, with enough elegance to settle in at the dinner table with grace. Buy by the case and enjoy from now until the holidays—this would be a nice choice for turkey and all the fixings.

HIGHLY RECOMMENDED

Daniel Lenko Estate Winery 2000 Rosé
Niagara Peninsula $

Another four-star finish for this refreshing and gentle rosé, which was also strongly recommended in the *Vines 2001 Buyer's Guide to Canadian Wine*. The tasters were unanimous in their praise for this tangy and slightly sweet rosé, which finishes with a very appealing lingering fruitiness. It's exactly the kind of wine that bartender Isaac Washington would serve alternately to the lovelorn and those in the first blush of romance aboard the *Love Boat*. This calls for a dry rosé!

Henry of Pelham Family Estate Winery 2001 Dry Rosé

Niagara Peninsula $ (395897)

Sour cherry, grapefruit and subtle earthy flavours make up the key descriptors for this bright, intense rosé. Made with the dinner table—or picnic basket—in mind, bursting with pure fruit flavour balanced by nice acid and some herbal notes. "It's zippy," remarked one favourable tasting note. When the thermostat rises, this is just the thing to serve as the first course of an amazing spring dinner party or with box lunches on a glorious Saturday afternoon in the park.

RECOMMENDED

Creekside Estate Winery 2001 Rosé

Niagara Peninsula $

Strawberry and melon notes are front and centre in this fuller-bodied rosé. Enjoy as a sipping wine or with a wide range of patio fare—from nacho chips to a posh selection of cheese. This is also a solid choice to pair with barbecued fare.

Hawthorne Mountain Vineyards 2000 Gamay Rosé Dry

Okanagan Valley $ (592980)

Here's a food-friendly rosé that pairs tart raspberry with some earthy strawberry notes to great effect. It's crisp with a slight herbal essence that adds some complexity to the flavour profile. The finish is nice and zesty, which makes this a good choice for grilled fish or fruit and cottage cheese.

Hillside Estate 2001 Gamay Blush

Okanagan Valley $$ (499848)

An interesting blend of Gamay and Auxerrois, this rosé has a lively strawberry zing to it. Fresh strawberry notes with pink grapefruit undertones carry onto the palate with a nice crisp acidity and dash of sweetness. Match with grilled freshwater fish or pork chops with wild rice.

Pillitteri Estates Winery 2000
Cabernet/Merlot Rosé
Niagara Peninsula $ (349217)
This delicious blended rosé flies in the face of anyone who considers pink wine to be simple and sweet. Complex aromas—mocha, strawberry, rhubarb—had panelists curling their toes with delight, while the flavourful and fruity palate inspired a blizzard of food pairings. Here the panel was split between those who see this as a fabulous aperitif wine and others who can't wait to pull the cork and serve it with hot, spicy Thai or Szechuan dishes.

Southbrook Winery 2000 Blush
Ontario $ (592220)
"Cherry fruit and cold cuts" was one descriptor of this curious, complex rosé that offers some of the appealing characteristics found in full-bodied red wines. Peppery, red berry fruit also figures in on the palate of this slightly sweet wine that finishes with a burst of earthy strawberry fruit. Serve with grilled pork chops, lamb or salmon burgers.

Sumac Ridge Estate Winery 2000
Okanagan Blush
Okanagan Valley $ (136994)
Fragrant aromas and pure fruit flavours are the hallmarks of this mouth-watering pink wine, which offers bountiful crushed red berry, citrus and lemon notes. On the palate, the fruit cocktail flavours are intense and well balanced. This is a clean, refreshing wine with a lasting finish. Good for dock, deck or dining room—there's isn't a summer setting where this blush would be out of place.

QUITE GOOD

Angels Gate Winery 2001 Rosé
Niagara Peninsula $

A suitably stirring debut vintage from a new Niagara producer, this is a wine that's clearly on the side of the angels. Deep lilac aromas marry with fresh raspberry and strawberry notes in this delicate rosé that's not too tart, not too sweet. A slight bitter nut note kept this ingenuous wine from scoring even higher marks from the panel.

Domaine Combret 1999 Cabernet Rosé
Okanagan Valley $$ (556340)

A solid choice for a sipping wine, this B.C. blush offers a hit of cherry cola and burst of strawberry in the whiff and taste. Good acidity balances the deep cherry and strawberry flavours. Chill and serve—or if you prefer, free the cork and your mind will follow.

Hawthorne Mountain Vineyards 1999 Gamay Rosé
Okanagan Valley $ (565143)

Pleasant fruit salad and green tea aromas delighted the whole panel, but the cloying sweetness on the palate was cause for concern for some. This Gamay Noir rosé is soft and flabby—it's best served as a sipping wine or would be an excellent base for sangria.

Hillebrand Estates 2001 Gamay Noir Rosé Vineyard Select
Niagara Peninsula $ (528455)

This refreshing rosé offers a hit of red berry fruit aromas along with some herbaceous notes. A solid summer sipper with a simple, brisk, crowd-pleasing style, Hillebrand's pinkie can entertain two or twenty. On a hot summer's night watching the sunset, what more are you looking for?

Stonechurch Vineyards NV Rosé Megan

Niagara Peninsula $ (569442)

Stonechurch has blended different grapes from different vintages to produce this floral and slightly candied rosé. Linden tree aromas and sour cherry fruit flavours dominate. This is a straightforward wine to enjoy this summer by the glass or with simple salads and corn on the cob.

Thirty Bench Wines 2000 Mountainview Blush

Niagara Peninsula $

A refreshing medium-dry blend of Vidal and Cabernet Franc, this is a deceptively pale rosé that possesses eye-opening intensity. Apricot and honey notes are among its obvious charms. On the palate, it's sweet but short. Serve with salads and Chinese food, especially chicken and pork dishes.

Thirty Bench Wines 1999 Trillium Blush

Niagara Peninsula $

The aroma of this wine is a dead ringer for red, white and blue popsicles—remember those icy cherry and strawberry wonders? Sweet and refreshing, this is too sticky for the dinner table. Poolside is more like it.

RED WINE

CABERNET FRANC

Cabernet Franc is one of the noble vinifera grape varieties particularly well suited to cool climate wine regions and is considered by many vintners to be Canada's great red hope. The hierarchy of Bordeaux red wines puts the leaner, more herbaceous Cabernet Franc a distant second to the heavyweight Cabernet Sauvignon. If the two grape varieties were personified by 1980s soul rock duo Hall and Oates, Cabernet Franc would be John Oates, the guy with the moustache who rode Daryl Hall's coattails to stardom.

In actuality, it's another case of a child surpassing its parent. In 1997, DNA research confirmed Cabernet Franc and Sauvignon Blanc were the parents of Cabernet Sauvignon.

Cabernet Franc, whose buds mature more than a week earlier than Cabernet Sauvignon, is lighter in colour and tannins than its more fashionable offspring. However, it has similar or higher levels of acidity and similar flavour and structure.

FOOD PAIRING SUGGESTIONS
Lamb, veal, beef tenderloin, London broils, venison burgers, grilled eggplant and portobello mushroom dishes, grilled vegetables, vegetarian lasagna, cheddar and other mild yellow cheeses, aged Stilton and Gorgonzola cheese.

Like other Bordeaux reds, its flavours tend more towards the salad bar spectrum (most notably green pepper) than juicy red fruit. One can detect raspberry when it is underripe or over-cropped, although in warm vintages such as 1998 and 1999 the wine can showcase a layered fruitiness that is extremely appealing.

According to Peninsula Ridge Estates winemaker Jean-Pierre Colas, the key to crafting spectacular Cabernet Franc is simple. "I want to put the grapes in the bottle," Colas said. That requires a stern hand in the vineyard to reduce yields, ensuring even ripening and the best possible grapes, and a deft touch with oak in the winery. "Varietal expression" are the watchwords for Colas, who says there's no point in making Cabernet Franc if it doesn't taste like Cabernet Franc. His reserve and barrel-aged Cabernet Franc are textbook examples: a little herbal note, a snap of lively acidity and a delicious core of fruit.

Franc-ly speaking, the grape is better known globally as a blending agent than the star of a one-grape wine. Adding Merlot and Cabernet Sauvignon helps fill in the holes of Cabernet Franc's lean structure to produce lush, mouthfilling wines. Cabernet Franc is the dominant grape in both Cheval Blanc, rightly considered one of Bordeaux's finest wines, and Viader, a California cult wine produced on Howell Mountain in Napa Valley. But the almost yearly success of one-grape Cabernet Franc in Ontario and British Columbia is nothing to shy away from.

The biggest hurdle to overcome is marketing. When consumers hear "Cabernet," they assume Cabernet Sauvignon is the topic at hand. Cabernet Franc produces truly great wines in France, particularly in the Loire and St-Emilion (Bordeaux) regions, but those are labelled as appellation or château wines. Only those wine lovers with a bit of Sherlock Holmes in them know they are enjoying premium Cabernet Franc.

The growing popularity of varietal Cabernet Franc in California will undoubtedly help cement the winning wine's reputation in the New World and help create a bigger market for these wonderful wines. Until then, consider yourself a pioneering force—the front line of Cabernet Franc fans who can reap the reward of being the first on the bandwagon.

Tasting Panel: LC, SD, SP, VP, CR, SS, WS, CW

VINES AWARD

Peninsula Ridge Estates Winery 2000 Reserve Cabernet Franc

Niagara Peninsula $$$

Wow. A rich, round model of Cabernet Franc with serious structure packed full of fruit flavours. Sweet spice and good varietal character—some earthy and tobacco notes enhance the generous mixed berry and currant flavours. It's a stand-out. The medium-bodied wine is dry and soft, but also rich and complex with a persistence of flavour that lingers. It is drinking nicely now and will cellar for five or more years. Enjoy with grilled swordfish or blackened fish, roast turkey or filet mignon with wild mushrooms.

Thirty Bench Wines 1999 Reserve Cabernet Franc Benchmark

Niagara Peninsula $$$$

This elegant and refreshing wine offers lovely ripe, crushed berry and floral scents. The spiciness of new oak and zest of youth punctuate its sweet mouth-filling flavours, which include blueberry, black olive and blackcurrant. Careful work in the vineyard results in an intense, deeply concentrated and age-worthy wine. This is truly a benchmark Cabernet Franc, which is worth the splurge for a special romantic dinner at home. Drink now to 2008. Serve with beef tenderloin or lamb, roasts, or fresh bread and olives.

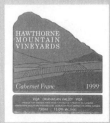

HIGHLY RECOMMENDED

Hawthorne Mountain Vineyards 1999 Cabernet Franc
Okanagan Valley $$ (593020)
A deliciously well-made Cabernet Franc. Although the 1999 growing conditions were on the cooler side, winemaker Bruce Ewert has managed to produce a concentrated wine that sparks of a classic Cab Franc. Heightened notes of fresh raspberry, cherry and strawberry flow from the glass. Integrated flavours of green pepper and red berry with a touch of sweet oak combine with a bright acidity and solid core of soft tannins in making this an elegant, food-friendly red.

Inniskillin Wines 1999 Cabernet Franc Reserve
Niagara Peninsula $$ (557389)
What a difference a year makes. Last year's tasting note suggested the wine's dusty tannins will soften to reveal a rich core of fruit and tasty spice and herbal flavours. Well, we were right. Delicious intense fruit and appealing mocha, leather and currant notes dominate the palate of this extremely tasty Cabernet Franc. Drink now to 2005.

Pillitteri Estates Winery 2000 Cabernet Franc
Niagara Peninsula $$ (349241)
A bold, rich and polished Cabernet Franc from a dedicated Niagara producer, with layers of earthy currant, spice, plum, smoke and toasty, spicy oak. A wonderfully delicious young wine, it will age gracefully. Drink now to 2006.

Strewn Wines 1999 Cabernet Franc
Niagara Peninsula $$ (582551)
A truly complex wine created by ideal growing conditions in 1999. Having reached full maturity in the vineyard, this Niagara grape's delicious

potential has been captured by winemaker Joe Will, who has constructed an expressive Cabernet Franc. Wonderful aromas of dried plum and cherry with a hint of anise carry over to the palate. With bright acidity and soft tannins, this wine is drinking exceptionally well now. Enjoy with heavier meat dishes or mushroom-based vegetarian meals.

Thirteenth Street Wine Co. 2000 Sandstone Cabernet Franc

Niagara Peninsula $$

Classic varietal character with herbaceous and dark berry notes. A plush core of fruit, good structure and excellent layers of fruit, oak and tannin that will knit together more seamlessly given a year or two in the bottle. Promises to be a knockout.

RECOMMENDED

Colio Estate Vineyards 1999 CEV Reserve Cabernet Franc

Lake Erie North Shore $$ (432096)

Lovely acidity keeps the concentrated plum and blackcurrant lively, and the long finish bodes well for the future. Medium-bodied, with silky tannins and nicely integrated toast elements.

Daniel Lenko Estate Winery 2000 Cabernet Franc

Niagara Peninsula $$

A nice intense, plush red, with well-focussed currant, pepper and herbal flavours and a nice toasted note. Herbal flavours linger on the finish. Decant, or let it air awhile. Plate up some cherry tomatoes and black olives over pasta and pour. You're in the zone.

Featherstone Estate Winery 2000 Unfiltered Cabernet Franc
Niagara Peninsula $

Smooth and seductive, this is Cabernet Franc in the vein of David Bowie. The captivating chocolate, mint and cherry character recalls Bowie's brooding, intense work on *Low* and *Heroes*. Elegant and well done, this is a great wine to savour over a late-night dinner by candlelight.

Featherstone Estate Winery 1999 Unfiltered Cabernet Franc
Niagara Peninsula $

Sweet, spicy components are the hallmarks of this structured and intense Cabernet Franc, with some cloves, vanilla, smoke and even butterscotch flavours. The acidity refreshes the spicy flavours on the finish. Drink now through 2004.

Hernder Estate Wines 1999 Cabernet Franc (Unfiltered)
Niagara Peninsula $ (399980)

A mix of sweet currant and raspberry flavours, with some meaty notes and tantalizing acidity. This pleasant, approachable wine is smooth and ready to drink. Enjoy with food—say, anything off the barbecue.

Hillebrand Estates 1999 Showcase Cabernet Franc Glenlake Vineyard
Niagara Peninsula $$$$ (994582)

A dark angel. Plum, black pepper and a dash of Bing cherry flavours combine with the sweet oak to create a supple, soft wine balanced out by a bright acidity. Not overly handled, this well-structured wine has all the elements of a classic Cabernet Franc. A hint of green pepper on the finish caps a wonderfully made wine.

Hillebrand Estates 1995 Showcase Cabernet Franc Unfiltered Glenlake Vineyard

Niagara Peninsula $$$$ (994582)

Mature Cabernet Franc offers aromas of chocolate, spice and everything nice in an aged red wine. For those of you keeping score at home, the list also includes leather, dried fruit, sweet tobacco, bread and mushrooms. Those earthy flavours carry over onto the palate and merge with some subtle currant fruit flavours for a nice layered mouthful. A bottle to impress clients or a date. Drink now.

Lakeview Cellars 2000 Cabernet Franc

Niagara Peninsula $$ (573220)

Consumer-friendly Franc with smoky raspberry and blackberry characters. Candied raspberry flavours with a touch of sweet oak. Bright acidity highlights the fruit tones with some medium tannins balancing the body. Drinking well now and could be paired with lighter white meat dishes or with a root vegetable stew.

Peller Estates 1999 Andrew Peller Signature Series Cabernet Franc Unfiltered

Niagara Peninsula $$$$ (981134)

When the winemaker coddles a wine, chances are good that the wine will express its inner self. This premium unfiltered red has been treated with a lot of TLC. Having spent some downtime in new oak, it has aromas of coffee, dark cherry and raspberry. Complex flavours of pepper, red berries and green pepper are encased by a lighter breeze of acidity with rounded tannins. Built to age for a few more years, this wine could be enjoyed now after a little while in the decanter.

Sandhill 2000 Cabernet Franc
Okanagan Valley $$ (556035)
The creation of Calona Wines Howard Soon and vineyard owner Richard Cleave, this premium wine is made from Burrowing Owl Vineyards fruit. Tender care and lower yields have rewarded the pair with a luscious red that is all about concentration. Ripe red berries jump out of the glass. On the palate, this fruit-driven red is enhanced by a small dose of sweet oak. Verging on full-bodied, it has enough acidity and tannins to carry through to its spicy finish. Relatively young in age, this wine will pair pleasurably with your favourite meat dishes, given a few years in the cellar or hours in a decanter.

Stonechurch Vineyards 1998 Cabernet Franc
Niagara Peninsula $$ (891051)
Selected as the red wine for the Royal Agricultural Winter Fair, this 1998 displays typical Cabernet Franc characters from a very warm growing season. Intense coffee, raspberry and blackcurrant flavours with supple tannins. Spicy black pepper finish rounds out a well-made wine.

Stoney Ridge Cellars 2000 Reserve Cabernet Franc Fox Vineyard
Niagara Peninsula $$ (433524)
A classic Cab Franc with typical pepper, cherry, and cassis notes. Rich, ripe and full of spice and red berry flavours, with a medium body. Capped by a lingering spicy finish. Match with pasta dishes, lamb chops or chili.

Stoney Ridge Cellars 1999 Bench Cabernet Franc
Niagara Peninsula $ (525691)
A medium-bodied red that would be a great match with grilled meats, fish and veggies. It's a versatile wine that has concentrated flavours of black pepper, plum and cassis. Firm tannins with a balanced acidity hold the flavours together through to a spicy finish. Drinking well now.

Stoney Ridge Cellars 1997 Cuesta Estates Cabernet Franc

Niagara Peninsula $$$$

Looking for an aged red wine that demonstrates Niagara's ability to produce wine with great age-ability? This wine would be worth a trip to Niagara. Crafted by winemaker Jim Warren during his tenure at Stoney Ridge, this Cab Franc is growing old gracefully. The fruit is now turning into dried plum with cassis berries. A velvety mouth-feel has been created by rounded tannins and the once bright acidity is now gently lifting the fruit. A peppery finish perfectly caps this six-year-old. Drinking well now, but it could have a few more years. An extravagant wine for a special evening.

Strewn Wines 2000 Cabernet Franc

Niagara Peninsula $ (557199)

Giving off intense aromas of figs, cherries and a little cedar, this wine is lighter in style on the palate, with a balanced acidity. Youthful but rounded tannins give an earthy texture to the dark fruit, with a hint of spicy green pepper on the finish. A classically made Cabernet Franc with enough depth to pair with seasoned meat or rich pasta dishes.

Strewn Wines 1999 Terroir Cabernet Franc

Niagara Peninsula $$ (582551)

Can you taste the "terroir" in the wine? A loaded term that has been the centre of much debate in the world of wine, Strewn's Terroir captures a unique take on Cabernet Franc. Ripe with red berry flavours, it also has undertones of green pepper and floral notes. A firm tannic body with bright acidity, full of fruit and herbal flavours. With a sweet touch up front and a hot spice finish, there's room for integration in the bottle over the next year or two. Attractive enough to enjoy now, but it will be better in time.

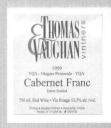

Thomas and Vaughan Vintners 1999 Cabernet Franc

Niagara Peninsula $$

An attractive offering with vanilla, cassis and pepper notes. Flavours of rich red berry with a touch of sweet oak give the wine an added texture. A lighter style with some acidity and youthful tannins. Best paired with white meats such as lamb.

QUITE GOOD

Ancient Coast 1999 Cabernet Franc

Niagara Peninsula $ (559195)

Some good fruit and a soft texture, but on the whole a one-dimensional wine. You sacrifice some taste for money here. Burger's up, cork's out. *Bon appétit.*

Château des Charmes Winery 1998 Cabernet Franc St. Davids Bench Vineyard

Niagara Peninsula $$ (453415)

A lighter offering that has the typical green pepper and cherry flavours. More herbal flavours on the palate with a spicy finish. This wine could be in the middle stages of aging. Decant for a while to allow the wine to fully express its different sides.

Harrow Estates 2000 Cabernet Franc

Lake Erie North Shore $ (297184)

A good burger or pizza wine, this is simple and light-bodied. Candied fruit and mint flavours are front and centre on the palate, which is rounded out by a noticeable but not unpleasant sweetness.

Harvest Estate Winery 2000 Cabernet Franc

Niagara Peninsula $

A fruity styled red with defined candied cherry and cedar aromas. A sweet oak touch on the palate heightens the cherry flavours with hints of pine and cedar. Built to be enjoyed now, there's no need to place this one in the cellar. Keep it in the kitchen rack for easy access.

Hillebrand Estates 1997 Showcase Cabernet Franc Unfiltered Glenlake Vineyard

Niagara Peninsula $$$ (399980)

Here's a big, burly Cabernet Franc, with complex aromas and flavours of hay, leather, earth and green pepper. The tannins are still raw and in need of taming, but the question is, will the appealing fruit flavours still be there when Father Time works his magic? Drink now, but be sure to decant an hour or two before serving.

Magnotta Wines 1999 Cabernet Franc Limited Edition

Niagara Peninsula $

Although it's not unpleasant, the fruit in this wine seems a little tired and green from such a warm harvest. Lean and structured like a Loire Valley Cabernet Franc, this has a good tug of tannin and some substance. Needs red meat to be truly happy.

Peller Estates 1999 Private Reserve Cabernet Franc

Niagara Peninsula $$ (981209)

A bit simple and rustic, but good ripe fruit on the palate and telltale green pepper notes. Full-bodied and pleasant, this is a wine to uncork and enjoy by itself or with a Greek feast.

Peller Estates 1998 Private Reserve Cabernet Franc

Niagara Peninsula $$ (981209)

Attractive chunky cherry fruit and dried herb aromas. Full-bodied and velvety, with a finish interrupted by a tannic grip. A bit tough and rustic, but good character. Needs food.

Strewn Wines 2000 Cabernet Franc Terroir Strewn Vineyard
Niagara Peninsula $$ (582551)

A good, simple red wine, with berry, currant and pepper character. Medium-bodied, with medium tannins and a light, fruity finish. The core of fruit and plush texture had more than one taster wondering if this could be a sleeper. Given some time in the bottle to integrate and harmonize, this could be a Highly Recommended wine.

Thirty Bench Wines 2000 Cabernet Franc Tradition
Niagara Peninsula $

"Tradition" in this case is code that the wine is unoaked, fermented and aged in stainless steel tanks, so what you taste is the true, unsullied character of Cabernet Franc grapes. The result is herbal, but tasty. Currants and leafy notes dominate and the finish is crisp and refreshing. This is a great food wine—serve with picnics and salads or grilled meat and vegetables.

Thomas and Vaughan Vintners 2000 Cabernet Franc
Niagara Peninsula $

This Cab Franc is just starting to spread its wings. It's a little young with its tight tannins and racy acidity. There's enough fruit dominated by plums and cassis to further develop as the wine ages. The toasty oak finish illustrates that the wine has yet to come to terms with its parts. A year together should integrate them and make this a fine wine.

Tinhorn Creek Vineyards 2000 Cabernet Franc
Okanagan Valley $$ (530717)

A youthful Cabernet Franc with tight cherry and raspberry flavours. Black pepper spice on the finish. Some time in the bottle should even out the fruit, acid and tannins. Decant for a while before serving with grilled tuna, smoked salmon and other spicy seafood dishes.

CABERNET SAUVIGNON

In the world of red wine, Cabernet Sauvignon is afforded the same fanatical popularity Chardonnay enjoys over less fashionable white wines. Cabernet Sauvignon is the reigning heavyweight champion of the world and has been down on all red varietal competitors for decades now. For many wine lovers, Cabernet Sauvignon is red wine to the exclusion of everything else on the wine list. We have California to thank for this. The surfer girls and surfer boys have turned the world onto one-grape Cabernet wines that deliver rousing fruit explosions on the palate. That movement has inspired many New World winemakers, including a strong Canadian contingent, to follow in their "go big or go home" wake.

But their Old World counterparts in Bordeaux continue to see the aristocratic grape variety as the King of Kings. Cabernet Sauvignon is the principal ingredient in their world-renowned blended reds, which often include smaller portions of

FOOD PAIRING SUGGESTIONS
This full-bodied red is a superb match for most hearty meat dishes—everything from roast beef, lamb and veal to a wild kingdom of caribou and duck. Vegetarians need not despair; powerful Cabernet is also an impressive partner with vegetable stews, tomato-based sauces and mushroom risotto.

Merlot, Cabernet Franc, Malbec and a few other earthy vinifera grapes.

A hearty grapevine with particularly hard wood, Cabernet Sauvignon thrives in vineyards in British Columbia and Ontario. Surviving the winter is rarely a problem, but getting the late-ripening grapes to full maturity can be. In exceptionally cold and difficult years, the wines can be weedy and hard, but in fine vintages they are delicious and wonderfully versatile. With back-to-back warm weather vintages in 1998 and 1999 and the cooler and more problematic 2000, the *Vines* panel saw the gamut of Cabernet Sauvignon styles—from salad bar green to lush and fruity.

Like the French approach, the main use of Cabernet Sauvignon in both provinces is as a blending agent for Cabernet-Merlot or Meritage wines. But given the beneficial growing conditions and in the right hands, it's not surprising that 100 per cent Cabernet Sauvignon wines are some of the best wines being produced in Canada. Classic Cabernet Sauvignon characteristics include cassis, redcurrant, mint, eucalyptus, black cherry, bell pepper and smoke.

Tasting Panel: DB, KR, WS, SS, CW, JW

HIGHLY RECOMMENDED

Inniskillin Wines 1999 Klose Vineyard Cabernet Sauvignon
Niagara Peninsula $$ (586297)
An excellent wine with real Cabernet character, Inniskillin's single-vineyard bottling offers complex notes of smoke, tobacco, leather and mint. Plum fruit flavours add some fleshiness to the palate, which is finely structured with nice, ripe tannins. The wine revealed more of its personality, the longer it was in the glass. Plan to decant before serving for best enjoyment. This wine should age beautifully.

**Mission Hill Family Estate Winery 1999
Reserve Cabernet Sauvignon**
Okanagan Valley $$ (553321)
A soft but solid Cabernet from one of Canada's
blue-chip wineries. This wine combines classic
Bordeaux character with the accessible, drink-it-
young plush fruit found in Cabernet from California
and Australia. Sweet berry fruit is balanced with
lots of complexity, including spice, black cherry,
intense leather and dried tobacco, and eucalyptus
notes. On the palate, it's so supple and so very
tasty. "Will age, but why wait?" was one taster's
remark. Indeed.

**Peller Estates 1999 Andrew Peller Signature
Series Cabernet Sauvignon**
Niagara Peninsula $$$$ (981126)
As one taster put it, "What's not to like?" A big,
mouth-filling Cabernet, Peller's luxury reserve deliv-
ers on all counts: depth and intensity of flavour,
complexity and, above all, the wow factor. This
aromatic wine offers nice earth, mint, tobacco,
leather spice and cedar notes, which yield to a
delicate core of slightly warm red cherry and red-
currant fruit flavours. The vibrant fruit is delicious
now, but one marvels at the potentially breath-
taking complexity likely to come with some bottle
age. A benchmark for the category.

**Peller Estates 1998 Private Reserve
Cabernet Sauvignon**
Niagara Peninsula $$ (981183)
An all-round good drinking Cabernet, Peller's
Private Reserve delivers sweet black cherry and
blueberry along with classic Cabernet flavours,
including tobacco, tar, dried herbs, menthol and
chocolate notes. The wine is very fruity, with a
soft, lingering finish. If you're looking to show off
the quality of Canadian red wine, it's hard to go
wrong with this one. Invite some friends and a big
steak or rustic cheese to the table and enjoy.

Quails' Gate Estate Winery 2000 Family Reserve Cabernet Sauvignon

Okanagan Valley $$$

This Cabernet is plump, concentrated and silky, with chocolate, mint and some leather notes. And with its plush tannins and deep red berry fruit, nicely supported with vanilla and toasty oak, it's a benchmark Canadian Cab. It's a standout within the category of so-called ultra-premium, luxury wines from British Columbia. The suppleness of the wine makes it easy to enjoy with a wide variety of food or none at all. It is delicious to drink and should age quite well, too.

Southbrook Winery 1999 Cabernet Sauvignon Lailey Vineyard

Niagara Peninsula $$ (448340)

A classic, classy Cab, this is a fabulous wine with an air of mystery about it. Nice soft perfume and smoke aromas—it smells a bit like Bogey, a bit like Bacall—and detailed complexity that surprised all tasters. Cedar, tar, meaty-smokiness, figs, dried spices and a core of black fruit make for a most appealing mouthful. All those exotic notes, you see, are borne on a fabulous frame, making this an excellent match for food. Although this wine definitely will improve with age, it's also nicely drinkable now.

RECOMMENDED

CedarCreek Estate Winery 1999 Cabernet Sauvignon Platinum Reserve

Okanagan Valley $$$ (607234)

Panelists loved the minty, cedary varietal character of this well-made Cabernet. The palate is very complex and intricately knit, but the abundance of oak character seems to overpower the black cherry and cassis fruit, which is a shame. The finish is long and seizes your senses.

Creekside Estate Winery 2000 Marcus Ansems Signature Cabernet Sauvignon

Niagara Peninsula $$$

This wine sparked debate among panelists, with some calling its earthy, meaty character deep and delicious. Others were decidedly underwhelmed. Fans of big, funky reds, such as rustic Rhône bottles or old school Bordeaux conveying a decidedly animal kick, will love this wine. Its plum and blackberry flavours combine with that earthy spiciness in a plush, mouth-filling wine. Definitely not to everyone's taste, but those who like it will savour its mysterious charms.

Hillebrand Estates 1999 Showcase Cabernet Sauvignon Glenlake Vineyard

Niagara Peninsula $$$$

This classically styled Cabernet Sauvignon, with subtle red berry fruit and some herbal notes, has excellent length and aging potential. It's got good concentration and substance and a savoury spice note that's extremely appealing.

Jackson-Triggs Okanagan Estate 2000 Cabernet Sauvignon Proprietors' Reserve

Okanagan Valley $$ (543884)

This is a sleeper. A very classy Cab, unencumbered by excessive oak and alcohol. The overwhelming consensus is that this wine has a five-star future. Right now, it's tannic and a little dumb, but the components are all there: soft, sweet cherry fruit, nice complexities, cedar and vanilla oak notes. Buy it now, but give it some time (and then invite us over to share in your good fortune).

Konzelmann Estate Winery 2000 Cabernet Sauvignon

Niagara Peninsula $$ (582312)

Here's a soft, ripe Cabernet recommended for everyday drinking for those who love plummy, rich reds. The palate is elegant and lean, but the fruit flavours are explosive. It's simple but special. Enjoy by the glass or with simple beef dishes or tomato-based sauces.

Lailey Vineyard 2000 Cabernet Sauvignon

Niagara Peninsula $$

A big, bold Cabernet with all the stuffing—cassis fruit, cedar smoke, vanilla and plush tannins. Fans of big reds should take note: there's deep spicy character to this wine, along with the more herbal spectrum of flavours one expects from a cooler vintage.

Peninsula Ridge Estates Winery 2000 Cabernet Sauvignon

Niagara Peninsula $$ (609800)

Concentrated damson plum and green pepper offers true-to-the-grape character. On the palate, the wine is soft with a long finish, with focussed flavours and a velvety texture. More than just yummy to drink, this is a rich, complex wine that offers a Zen moment of enjoyment.

Peninsula Ridge Estates Winery 2000 Cabernet Sauvignon Reserve

Niagara Peninsula $$$

This wine has real Cabernet varietal character without a lot of oak notes, and succeeds thanks to its plum and tobacco flavour seasoned with a touch of earth and a tug of tannin. Great structure and well balanced, this is a very versatile food wine.

Reif Estate Winery 2000 Cabernet Sauvignon
Niagara Peninsula $$ (304162)
An expressive Cabernet with sweet fruit and vanilla custard dominating the profile. The plummy fruit aromas are engaging. On the palate, a spicier character takes over. Firm tannins give the body a bit of a boost. The red winemaking at Reif seems to get better every year. This wine has great age-ability for anyone looking for an inexpensive cellar dweller.

Strewn Wines 2000 Cabernet Sauvignon Terroir Strewn Vineyard
Niagara Peninsula $$ (529693)
There's a decided snap to the flavour punch this wine delivers. Easy and enjoyable, there's a sweet cherry pop to the palate, which also features generous chocolate and rich currant flavours. This is a wine to enjoy by the glass, say, when watching *Fight Club* or *Ali*.

Strewn Wines 1998 Cabernet Sauvignon Terroir Strewn Vineyard
Niagara Peninsula $$ (557082)
The tasting note, "Geez ..." could go either way, but when the panelist had just noted this wine's prodigious chocolate, plum, cassis and sweet caramel notes, that's pretty close to a rave review. Those tasty characters are met with some stemmy, herbal notes, which took some of the sheen off this tasty, impressive Cabernet.

Sumac Ridge Estate Winery 1998 Black Sage Vineyard Cabernet Sauvignon
Okanagan Valley $$ (392373)
An all-round good drinking Cabernet, this wine puts its focus on the fruit. A big, soft palate delivers vanilla oak, rich plummy fruit, and some subtle tobacco and spice notes. The silky, smooth texture makes this a no-brainer for entertaining. It will please a wide variety of palates.

QUITE GOOD

Château des Charmes Winery 1999 St. Davids Bench Vineyard Cabernet Sauvignon

Niagara Peninsula $$ (453423)

The deeply concentrated cassis, violet and licorice notes are terrific, but there's a dirty note on the nose that had tasters scratching their heads. (Another bottle carried the same funky note.) The palate recovers with loads of fruit and delicate spice. Enjoy now to 2008.

Daniel Lenko Estate Winery 2000 Cabernet Sauvignon

Niagara Peninsula $$

A peppery, fruity and crowd-pleasing style of Cabernet that is both smooth and savoury. Well balanced and easy drinking, with abundant blue plum and some leafy tobacco notes on the palate. It will develop in the bottle, but there's no reason to wait.

Lakeview Cellars 2000 Cabernet Sauvignon Reserve

Niagara Peninsula $$ (618793)

Winespeak is easy to parody, but if you want to know what tasters mean by "velvety texture," try this subtle yet complex Cab. The mouth-feel is plush and packed with cherry and berry fruit and spice. This wine offers a nice balance of Cabernet's soft and tough qualities.

Magnotta Wines 2000 Cabernet Sauvignon

Niagara Peninsula $

Bright cranberry and mint aromatics make for a pleasing introduction to this lean but elegant Cabernet Sauvignon. Some positive bell pepper and cedar forest notes add complexity to the palate. Enjoy with fall and winter stews or other hearty beef dishes.

Marynissen Estates 2000 Cabernet Sauvignon
Niagara Peninsula $$

It's too early to judge this dense, tight Cabernet, which has some powerful fig and prune notes and more earthy character than most. Having good structure and some substance, this wine will likely yield more impressive results when we taste it next year.

Stonechurch Vineyards 2000 Cabernet Sauvignon
Niagara Peninsula $ (353318)

Deep earthy and olive notes are interesting though not unpleasant. On the palate, the wine is lean and herbal with some chewy currant character. Best with soft cheeses or simple barbecued fare.

Stonechurch Vineyards 1998 Cabernet Sauvignon Reserve
Niagara Peninsula $$$ (591842)

Nice, though not particularly expressive of Cabernet character, this would be a crowd pleaser as a simple red. Soft and ripe, there's a lot of positive flavour here. Enjoy with holiday dinners or to mark special anniversaries.

Thomas and Vaughan Vintners 1999 Cabernet Sauvignon Estate Reserve
Niagara Peninsula $$

Toasted oak barrels have lent this wine a definite campfire scent, which had tasters recalling long, hot summers on Lake Simcoe, canoeing, sailing and generally lazing the summer away. Nice memories to be sure, but the burnt note dominates the wine. Sweet vanilla and a plush mouthfeel add to the enjoyment.

CABERNET BLENDS

To best describe why winemakers blend red varieties, we decided to pull a buzzword from the business pages of the daily newspapers: "convergence." For some varieties, most notably Cabernet Sauvignon, Merlot and Cabernet Franc, there is a synergy of flavours and structure that produce a better, fuller wine than any one-grape wine. The sum is, indeed, better than its parts. If only AOL and Time-Warner blended as seamlessly.

There is, however, no formula, no secret recipe for vintners to follow when blending red wines. Winemakers must sweat out the process, tasting every barrel in the cellar to produce their vintage wine. Bordeaux winemakers have been blending Cabernet and Merlot, along with Malbec and Petit Verdôt, for centuries, which is why some Canadian wineries refer to their red blends as "Bordeaux blends." The French figured out long

FOOD PAIRING SUGGESTIONS
Blended reds offer a more diverse package for pairing with foods. Many of the wines reviewed in this section would be best suited for hearty meals. From stews and chili to steaks and roasts, most red meats would stand up to the blends. As well, some of the lighter blends could be paired with white meat such as pork and lamb. For vegetarians, try spicy pastas or grilled veggies with a nice hearty red.

ago that working with a variety of compatible grapes is the best insurance against disease and uneven ripening in the vineyard. The winemaker then has the flexibility to blend the harsh tannins and acidity of underripe Cabernets with the softer and richer flavours of Merlot, which ripens much earlier in the season. The percentage of each variety changes from year to year to reflect the strong suits of every vintage.

Like single varietal wines, blends vary widely in style, quality and price. The range submitted for tasting spanned to the highest tier of Canadian wine, with many bottles priced at $35 or more. These are expensive wines to make. The judicious vineyard cropping required to reduce yields and guarantee the ripest possible fruit, and the expense of long-term aging in costly oak barrels, means that serious Bordeaux blends come with an equally serious price tag.

Be that as it may, it should be noted here that Canadian blended reds consistently outshine stand-alone Cabernet Sauvignon or Merlot. We hope that more wineries will turn to blending to make the very best big reds instead of focussing so much attention on stand-alone varietals, which need exceptionally warm growing seasons to thrive.

The process isn't confusing, but the wine labelling practice invariably is. Why are some wines labelled as Meritage (a California moniker for a Bordeaux blend wine, which rhymes with "heritage"), while some are Cabernet-Merlot and others still are given proprietary names such as Nota Bene, Trius Red or Oculus? Good question, and one that Canadian winemakers should address so the system can be demystified for confused consumers.

Tasting Panel: JI, BS, GP, WS, CW

VINES AWARD

Mission Hill Family Estate Winery 1999 Oculus
Okanagan Valley $$$ (572032)
A wine suited to match its visionary name. Oculus is a fresh, fleshy New World blend (insider code for loads of enjoyable fruit minus the overbearingly tannic grip and funky notes found in classically French wines), this full-bodied red is one of the best wines crafted in Canada to date. Huge potential, with good, rich fruit concentration, this wine offers vibrant blackberry and raspberry fruit and nuances of blueberry, green pepper and black pepper. Packed with a rich core of fruit and balanced with a pleasant astringency, it will drink well over the next six years. Serve with red meat, pasta or grilled poultry.

Vineland Estates Winery 1999 Meritage
Niagara Peninsula $$$$
Vineland Estates created quite a stir when it slapped the $125 price tag on its signature red wine. Its wine created quite a stir with our panelists, who, tasting it blind, had no idea of the wine's price or pedigree. They just knew they were in love or, in the words of one panelist, "had the floor ripped out from underneath them." Intense, complex aromas—perfume, violets and some plum pudding—pave the way for a fruit-packed palate, which is countered with some young tannins. Excellent concentration. This is as stylish, complex and thoroughly magical as anything from Bordeaux in its price class.

HIGHLY RECOMMENDED

Black Hills Estate Winery 2000 Nota Bene
British Columbia $$$ (708073)
Big red fans will want to take note of Nota Bene. A seriously good, serious Cabernet blend that delivers high-intensity red fruit and fine-grained structure that will develop and open up in time. The aromas are a little reserved at present, but there's enough amazing fruit concentration to make this a slam dunk.

Château des Charmes Winery 2000 Cabernet-Merlot
Niagara Peninsula $ (454991)
A classically styled blend of forty-five per cent Cabernet Sauvignon, forty-three per cent Cabernet Franc and twelve per cent Merlot, this bargain-priced wine over-delivers on quality and value. Jammed with currant and berry goodness, it has a plush mouth and rich texture. This is one to buy by the case, as the wine is delectable now, and will continue to round out in the cellar over the next one to two years. Best Buy.

Henry of Pelham Family Estate Winery 1999 Cabernet-Merlot
Niagara Peninsula $$$ (395885)
Good and gripping right now, this wine promises to be a stand-out given some time in the bottle. Some attractive fruit and wood notes, with intensity that's not huge, but deep and pleasurable. Equally pleasurable is the complex, full-bodied palate, packed full of fruit, with the alcohol and astringency supporting the incredible weight. This will age and open up. Drink 2004 to 2010. In other words, wait for the video release.

Hillebrand Estates 1999 Trius Grand Red

Niagara Peninsula $$$$ (981050)

The debut vintage of Hillebrand's new ultra-premium red is surprisingly approachable in its relative youth. A special barrel selection of the three blending wines was undertaken to maximize structure and flavour. Ripe fruit from the warm 1999 harvest was mellowed and enhanced through long-term aging in small oak *barriques* and gains complexity from some tobacco and leafy notes. Young ripe tannins and a lovely, lush mouth-feel promise this wine will be a future star.

Peninsula Ridge Estates Winery 2000 Reserve Merlot-Cabernet

Niagara Peninsula $$$

A Gene Kelly kind of wine, with a powerful persistence of flavour, but also a smart elegance to its structure that recalls the athletic yet graceful star *of Singing in the Rain*. Light to medium-bodied, with a gentle red-berry bouquet, this blend of Merlot (fifty-five per cent) and Cabernet Sauvignon (forty-five per cent) is soft and balanced, the rough edges polished out by way of months aging in oak barrels. Nicely integrated oak supports the fruit and points it in the right direction. Ready to drink now, this is splendid with roast chicken or garlicky tapas.

Vineland Estates Winery 2000 Meritage

Niagara Peninsula $$$$

Another Vineland crackerjack Meritage, the 2000 delivers fine oak notes, a slightly leafy character and dense Christmas pudding aromas. A mellow mouthful, its hedonistic charm comes from its dense core of perfectly ripened fruit. Enjoyable now, this will improve in your cellar. Drink 2005 to 2008 for best enjoyment.

RECOMMENDED

Cave Spring Cellars 2000 Cabernet-Merlot
Niagara Peninsula $$
Complex fruit and some green pepper notes stand out. On the palate, there's wonderful fruit intensity, some sweet notes and a nice lingering finish. Excellent food wine. Best enjoyed with traditional *coq au vin*, roast beef with horseradish or roasted rack of lamb.

Cave Spring Cellars 1998 Cabernet-Merlot Beamsville Bench
Niagara Peninsula $$$ (316943)
Twists of tobacco and cracked pepper wind their way through this generous red wine. A little tart, but with the right meal, say a lean cut of beef and grilled veggies, this wine would be right at home.

Colio Estate Vineyards 1999 CEV Cabernet/Merlot Signature
Lake Erie North Shore $$$$ (612853)
Lighter style, but complex with interesting flavours and vanilla finish. Deep oak spice from long-term aging in French oak barrels and attractive savoury aromas adding to the enjoyment.

Harrow Estates 2000 Cabernet-Merlot
Lake Erie North Shore $ (432054)
This Cabernet Franc–dominant blend has generous black pepper and plum notes blending with the oak spice and smoke on the nose. There's a rich, ripe mouth-feel that pits berry fruit against some cedary spice and yields a tasty and complex wine. Enjoy with mushroom-flavoured dishes and gourmet burgers with grilled portobellos.

Hernder Estate Winery 1999 Meritage Estate Unfiltered

Niagara Peninsula $$$ (572560)

The debut edition of Hernder's high-end wine is a traditional blend of the Big Three: Cabernet Sauvignon, Merlot and Cabernet Franc. Generous fruit flavours are enhanced and pointed in the right direction by supple oak notes, which also impart a lingering vanilla lilt to the wine. Nice and lush, this is a big red for big red meat dinners. Steak ahoy!

Hester Creek Vineyards 2000 Cabernet-Merlot

Okanagan Valley $ (524678)

Clearly concentrated and rich, showing delicious Dutch licorice, cedar and grilled vegetable aromas and earthy, spicy fruit flavours. Smooth and supple, enjoy by the glass or with an assortment of aged Canadian cheddars.

Hillebrand Estates 1997 Trius Red

Niagara Peninsula $$$ (303800)

This complex wine with some mature Cabernet character presents positive cedar, leather and spice nuances that overflow the bowl of the wineglass. Moderate fruit and balanced acidity make for an enjoyable, food-friendly classic Bordeaux-style wine. Drink now to 2005.

Inniskillin Okanagan Vineyards 1999 Reserve Meritage

Okanagan Valley $$ (558395)

Exotic and rich, with a wide array of flavours—layers of smoke, chocolate, ripe cherry, vanilla, dried tobacco and hazelnut—and a creamy, full palate. Screams out for steak and mushrooms. Best from 2002 to 2006.

Inniskillin Wines 1999 Reserve Meritage
Niagara Peninsula $$ (558056)
Rich in flavour, firm in style, this wine presents attractive leather and currant notes framed by chewy tannins. Best after 2003 or decant and partner with a rib steak or lamb chops.

Jackson-Triggs Niagara Estate 1999 Meritage Proprietors' Grand Reserve
Niagara Peninsula $$ (594002)
This blend of Cabernet Sauvignon (fifty per cent), Merlot (thirty-five per cent) and Cabernet Franc (fifteen per cent) features positive berry fruit and nice oak complexity underscored by firm, dry tannins. Good intensity and concentration. Enjoy with beef tenderloin or white fish, or chicken in a red-wine reduction.

Maleta Vineyards 1999 Meritage
Niagara Peninsula $$
Deep and lovely, this wine offers a good fruity mouthful of flavours, including chocolate, dark fruit and cedar. The palate is full bodied and mouth filling. Pair with meat-based casseroles and other hearty dishes.

Peninsula Ridge Estates Winery 2000 Cabernet
Niagara Peninsula $
Complex texture and structure, with a hint of licorice, pepper and cherry and redcurrant fruit. The polished, stylish palate features good fruit intensity, integrated tannins and earthy tea flavours on the finish.

Reif Estate Winery 2000 Meritage Estate Bottled
Niagara Peninsula $$
This sleek and supple blend of Cabernet Sauvignon and Merlot offers rich tobacco, berry and vanilla notes. Generous palate, with moderate

richness and complexity, it shows a lot of character for not a lot of money. The fresh berry fruit flavour lingers on the palate and makes for an extremely enjoyable wine that's both approachable now and age worthy.

Southbrook Winery 1999 Triomphe Cabernet-Merlot

Niagara Peninsula $$$ (533299)

Bold and ripe, with promising layers of cola, smoke, coconut and rich black cherry flavours flowing across the palate before the tannins weigh in. The wine is soft and full-flavoured, with big oak notes and attractive savoury and coffee character on the long, long finish. Drink now to 2008.

Strewn Wines 1998 Three Terroir

Niagara Peninsula $$$ (468918)

This smooth, ripe Cabernet blend is low keyed at first blush. Bright acidity streamlines the palate, which is creamy and smacks of sweet oak spice. Subtle herbal notes harmonize with blackberry and vanilla.

Sumac Ridge Estate Winery 1998 Pinnacle

Okanagan Valley $$$$ (593061)

Well-made, Merlot-dominant blend, with chocolate, cigar box, sage and thyme aromas preceding flavours of vanilla and currants, finishing a bit raw. It's too young to drink now without decanting for an hour or so before dinner. Its intense chocolate tones would complement dark bittersweet chocolate truffles for an unconventional yet memorable pairing.

Vineland Estates Winery 2000 Reserve Cabernet-Merlot

Niagara Peninsula $$$

This almost fifty/fifty partnership between Cabernet Sauvignon and Merlot benefits from deep blackberry, cherry and raspberry aromas. The fruit has been plumped up by fourteen months in French oak barrels, which is responsible for the pretty undertones of herbs and vanilla. Best from 2003 to 2008.

QUITE GOOD

Creekside Estate Winery 2000 Laura's Blend

Niagara Peninsula $$ (572180)

Laura's Blend is wine with complexity, tannic strength and solid potential. The fruit is cloaked by oak notes at present. The finish is fresh and shows good balance.

EastDell Estates Winery 2000 Cabernet-Merlot

Niagara Peninsula $

Nice spice and complex oak character are featured in this straightforward red. Sweet fruit on the palate makes this an enjoyable sipping wine.

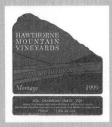

Hawthorne Mountain Vineyards 1999 Meritage

Okanagan Valley $$ (593004)

Firm, with focussed vanilla and currant flavours mingling with young tannins on the finish. Serve with a rustic meal of smoked meats, crusty bread and cheeses.

Mission Hill Family Estate Winery 2000 Cabernet/Merlot

Okanagan Valley $ (257816)

Interesting aromatics, including smoked veggie burger and eucalyptus notes. Big oak and moderate fruit flavour makes for a rather woody character. This wine has the right stuff to stare down a choice of beef or veal.

Sumac Ridge Estate Winery 1999 Cabernet/Merlot

Okanagan Valley $ (551911)

Round and accessible, with lush berry and cherry and pretty oak undertones. Enjoy with red meats and tomato-based pasta dishes.

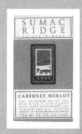

Thirteenth Street Winery Co. 2000 Sandstone Meritage

Niagara Peninsula $$

Nice fruit and autumn leaf aroma. The elegant palate shows richness, some smoke and a range of salad bar flavours. Drink now to 2007.

Thirty Bench Wines 1999 Benchmark Merlot Cabernet Sauvignon Cabernet Franc Reserve

Niagara Peninsula $$$$

A leaner wine than the price or producer would suggest. Thirty Bench has a cult following for its big-boned red wines, which are generally bigger and lusher than this delicate offering. Some pleasant fruit and complex notes, but they cannot contain the hot alcohol and bright acidity found on the palate. Drink now.

Thirty Bench Wines 1999 Cabernet-Merlot Tradition

Niagara Peninsula $$

What makes this wine is the intensity of fruit aromas and flavours—tasters gushed about the wine's chocolate plum and strong berry notes. The palate delivers a hint of sweetness along with the fruit, but the wine tastes a bit out of whack.

Thomas and Vaughan Vintners 1999 Meritage

Niagara Peninsula $$

Some herbal salad bar elements and tobacco mingle with the core of red fruit flavours, adding some complexity and depth. Pleasant and rich on the palate, finishing with the sizzle of a little alcohol heat. Enjoy over the next two years, with or without food.

MERLOT

There were two bottles on the table—one was a Merlot, the other was a Cabernet, and at the end of the night there were three bottles of the Merlot left. I tell ya, Merlot gets no respect! The Rodney Dangerfield of the wine world, Merlot is forever being passed over for Cabernet—Franc and Sauvignon.

The role that has been assigned to Merlot is that of supporting cast. In France, Merlot is widely planted, not to be produced as a single varietal, but to support the Bordeaux blends, which include Cabernet Sauvignon, Cabernet Franc and Merlot. Forever living in the shadow of the Cabernet giants, Merlot counters the highly tannic structure of Cabernet Sauvignon and its supple fruit and sweeter characteristics balance the Cabernets to make the blended red approachable in its youth.

On its own, a well-made Merlot can display supple fruit—such as black cherries, cassis and

FOOD PAIRING SUGGESTIONS
The more complex, full-bodied Merlots would go well with red meats. The lighter-styled versions would be good companions with pork roast, duck, quail and other game birds.

raspberries—with a touch of sweetness. It can handle oak, and if a deft hand is used in the process, chocolate and tobacco mingle with the fruit, giving the wine more complexity.

In Canada, Merlot is living a double life. The early flowering and ripening characteristics of the varietal makes it an appealing red grape to produce. Widely grown in both British Columbia and Ontario, the grape is being used by wineries for both a blending wine and single varietal production. The consistent success of its blending capabilities can be witnessed in the Cabernet Blends section of the book. As a one-grape wine, the results vary widely.

In just a few years, Merlot had gone from dazzling to dismal. This wasn't just a Canadian problem; it was an everywhere problem. Producers in California, New Zealand, Washington State, Chile, France and elsewhere, really lost the plot when it came to making Merlot. Merlot suffered the same fate that befell Chardonnay in the earlier decade—it was a victim of its own success. With few exceptions, unless you were paying $40 or more for your Merlot, you were buying over-oaked plonk. Even with the exceptions, there was no guarantee of actually getting the gorgeous fruit and velvety, soft texture that makes Merlot such a satisfying drink.

Canada is now elevating Merlot back to its once-lofty heights. This year's tasting panel was pleasantly pleased after tasting more than sixty Merlots. The *Vines* Award winner, Mission Hill's 1999 Merlot, stands on top of a very impressive group of wines. "It's rewarding to know that our hard work and risk-taking has paid off," explained John Simes, winemaker for Mission Family Estate Winery. "The '99 vintage was unusually cool for the Okanagan Valley, so we were forced to cut our yield down even further than normal to maintain the concentration in the fruit. We actually had to crop down twice because the weather was just not cooperating." The result was a great wine from a below-average vintage. A true sign that, while it's easy to make a great wine in an ideal growing season, the mark of a great winemaker comes from producing standout wines in a subpar growing season.

With most Merlots coming from the 1999 and 2000 vintages, there is a level of consistency starting to develop as the Merlot vines in Canada are getting more mature and winemakers are adapting to the vineyards with better results each year. The jury is still out on domestic Merlot's ability to win an Oscar for a leading role. However, there are bright spots where Merlot shines, and an Oscar is an Oscar. An exceptional supporting role is just as important as carrying a film alone.
Tasting Panel: DB, RD, WS, CW

VINES AWARD

Mission Hill Family Estate Winery 1999 Merlot
Okanagan Valley $$ (496109)
Every once in a while, you taste a wine and say to yourself, this can't be Canadian. As Canadians we're taught to think this way about everything from music to film to literature. We've been programmed to think that if it's really good, it can't be a Canadian product. And Canadian wine has an even tougher row to hoe because of its humble past. So, when the panel tasted Mission Hill's 1999 Merlot, it was hard for us to believe it indeed came from a Canadian producer. Lush notes of blueberry and vanilla filled the glass. Wonderful flavours of blueberry, blackcurrant and hints of pine and cedar illustrate its complexity. Warm, soft and supple, this Merlot has it all. It's the complete package, from the opening note to the last drop. Believe it or not, this wine could easily stand beside Australian, California and Washington State Merlot.

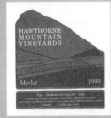

HIGHLY RECOMMENDED

Hawthorne Mountain Vineyards 1999 Merlot
Okanagan Valley $ (440701)
This was described fittingly by a panelist as a
"wide" wine. It's like travelling down a winding
two-lane road that suddenly opens up to four
lanes. The rush of speed and space is exhilarating.
This wine is like that sudden surge. It opens with
cherry, raspberry and cedar notes. On the palate,
it takes off with a rush of soft tannins and flavourful red berries, with an added touch of peppery
spice. A lengthy finish maintains the space and
leaves the senses tingling in anticipation of the
next surge. Move over Sunday drivers, this wine's
for those with a need for speed—or meaty pastas
and spicy sausages.

Henry of Pelham Family Estate Winery 1999 Merlot
Niagara Peninsula $$ (291120)
There's something about sitting in the dark near
the warm glow of a crackling fire that inspires the
urge to uncork a deep, dark red. Maybe it's the
flights of remembering, or forgetting, or just a
desire to reflect. This Merlot would be the perfect
companion on such an evening. Smoky, with
notes of bumbleberry and cedar giving way to
flavours of deep dark berries with a touch of
vanilla. Its long, soft finish with supple tannins
makes for a wonderful wine to contemplate the
"if" in life.

Hester Creek Estate Winery 2000 Merlot
Okanagan Valley $$
Although a tank sample was submitted to the
tasting because the winery was waiting for bottles
to arrive, it's a stunning example of Merlot. Hugely
extracted, it has aromas of chocolate, cedar, mint

and cherry. Its flavour profile is more of currants and cedar. The tannins are intrusive, yet firm with round edges, but they point to a wine that will stand the test of time. A sweet touch from the oak complements the fruit. Wait for the next couple of years for this Merlot to shine.

Peninsula Ridge Estates Winery 2000 Merlot
Niagara Peninsula $$ (592261)
Expressive yet restrained—think Kevin Spacey in *American Beauty*. Cassis, blueberry and blackcurrant notes foreshadow the flavours of this wine. A robust mouth-feel with firm but integrated tannins and a nice streak of acidity that holds the flavours of the wine through to its finish. Although hints of a monster red lurk in this Merlot, the winemaker did an excellent job of taming the beast. Drinking well know, but it could hold for a few years.

Pillitteri Estates Winery 1999 Merlot Reserve
Niagara Peninsula $$ (349258)
Winemaker Sue-Ann Staff has a deft hand with reds. The recent winner of the 2002 Ontario Wine Awards as Winemaker of the Year, Staff has established a track record of producing plush reds year after year. Her Merlot Reserve is no exception. Generous notes of plum, tobacco and leather, with a whiff of cedar. Upfront tannins play to the size of the wine. Big and bold without being abrasive. Flavours of dark berries with an earthy coating add to the wine's complexity. Needs time to fully integrate, but if you're in a hurry, decant for an hour before serving. This could handle robust meat dishes and would fit in nicely around a good game of poker.

Sumac Ridge Estate Winery 1999 Merlot
Okanagan Valley $ (593079)

"Penetrating," a simple word that captures the essence of this wine. Full of coffee, cedar, mint and cassis notes, this Merlot has more character than most Hollywood movies. A plush palate with flavours of blueberry, tea and vanilla, with rounded tannins balanced by an even acidity throughout the wine. Lingering finish highlights a well-designed wine—one that doesn't cost millions to make. Built for grilled dishes or Cuban cigars on the porch.

Sumac Ridge Estate Winery 1998 Merlot Black Sage Vineyard
Okanagan Valley $$ (392407)

This wine was conceived from an overly hot growing season in the Valley. With heightened concentration, the wine has intense aromas of smoky coffee, spices and a blend of raspberry and cassis. Deep, delicious fruit flavours go to the core of the wine. With softened tannins and a lingering richness, this is a classic example of a well-made Merlot from an unusual growing season. Keep around in the cellar for a few more years, or enjoy the fruits of a great wine now.

Wild Goose Vineyards 2000 Merlot
Okanagan Valley $ (497305)

Some reds are destined to be aged in cellars for years, others are best consumed within a few years of their creation. This Merlot falls somewhere in between. Attractive notes of chocolate and cherry give way to a plush, flavourful wine. Cherry and vanilla flavours are rounded out by a soft, velvety texture enhanced by a touch of sweet oak. The finish accents some aggressive tannins, but decanting before dinner should soften it. Match with roasts, dishes from the grill and pasta.

RECOMMENDED

Cave Spring Cellars 1998 Merlot

Niagara Peninsula $$$ (235051)

A stellar wine from the 1998 vintage, touted as one of the best on record for wineries in Ontario, although it's a debatable claim given the 1999 and 2000 vintage results. This Merlot shows that a little time in the bottle is a good thing. Wafts of coffee, blueberry and vanilla carry through to the palate. It's still hanging on to its bright fruit, enhanced by a softened acidity and rounded tannins. A great wine to uncork now, but still decant to allow the wine to open up from its long slumber in the bottle. Rich, heavy meats would be the ideal matches—or earthy grilled veggies.

Château des Charmes Winery 1999 Merlot St. Davids Bench Vineyard

Niagara Peninsula $$$ (453431)

This one is a big, beefed-up red with loads of interesting characters. Meaty notes mixed with spices, raspberries and tart cherries. On the palate, it's spicier than most New World Merlots, but there's enough fruit to level out its more earthy textures. Velvety mouth-feel, firm tannins and lengthy finish give this Merlot a brawny appeal that would be most enjoyed by those looking for a little might in their red. It's the Mighty Mouse of Merlots.

Creekside Estate Winery 2000 Marcus Ansems Signature Series Merlot
Niagara Peninsula $$$$

Aussie winemaker Marcus Ansems has a knack for getting the most out of his reds. Ansems is like an abstract artist as he crafts his wines in the cellar. His signature Merlot is a unique big red with smoky barnyard notes and plum and cassis hanging around. Huge flavours of plum and dark cherry are balanced between streaks of acidity and firm tannins. Although heavily smoked from the oak, this wine was built to age. No need to release this wine from the cellar for a few years, and even when doing so, give it a lot of time to breath. A work of art.

Harvest Estate Wines 1999 Merlot
Niagara Peninsula $ (579987)

If you're looking for a wine to uncork and drink, this one should do just fine. Attractive chocolate, vanilla and blueberry aromas showcase friendly attributes of a well-made wine. Cinder wood, blueberry and strawberry are lifted by a rich, round mouth-feel. The tannins are a little firm, but this wine was crafted to drink now. Full of flavours, this is an affordable Merlot that doesn't need to get acquainted with the cellar.

Hillebrand Estates 1999 Showcase Merlot Glenlake Vineyard
Niagara Peninsula $$$ (994574)

If a tree falls in the forest, what would it smell like? It could smell like this wine, with its pine, cedar and herbal notes. Deep earthy flavours with a soft, rounded texture. Hints of blueberry and a touch of sweet vanilla add to the wine's attractiveness. A lingering finish of peppery spice with firm tannins makes for a great food wine. Still a little youthful, it could use a few more years of downtime.

Hillside Estate 2000 Merlot Reserve
Okanagan Valley $$$ (536839)
Expressive fruit is the key to this wine's success.
Bright Bing cherry, raspberry and currant float
effortlessly from the glass. The big fruit explodes
on the palate with a touch of sweet oak. Solid
tannins with a medium intensity that carries the
wine to a leathery finish. Give this one a year or
two to round out its edges.

**Jackson-Triggs Okanagan Estate 2000
Merlot Proprietors' Reserve**
Okanagan Valley $$ (543876)
Like a lily greeting the early morning sun, the
longer this wine sits in the glass, the more expressive it becomes. Attractive notes of cassis, vanilla
and blueberry point to a nicely extracted wine
from a hot vintage. A heavy oak hand interrupted
the flavours, but after some time in the bottle, the
oak should integrate into the blush of fruit. Young
tannins will also soften up. Keep the cork in the
wine for the next three years, or let it breath for a
few hours before serving.

**Jackson-Triggs Okanagan Estate 1999 Merlot
Proprietors' Grand Reserve**
Okanagan Valley $$ (572040)
Wonderfully aromatic with hints of coffee, cassis
and vanilla with a touch of mint. A hint of sweet
oak on the palate with red berry flavours, all held
together by firm tannins. A spicy finish caps this
wine, deserving of its reserve tag. Although it
could use a few more years to allow for full
integration, it is drinking well now. Reserve for a
special dinner—or offer as a great gift for those
who love flavourful reds.

Konzelmann Estate Winery 2000 Merlot Reserve

Niagara Peninsula $ (439281)

A reserve wine that is drinking very well now. It's full of heady aromas of raspberry, vanilla and chocolate. Flavours of cocoa and raspberry are lifted by velvety tannins and balanced acidity. Approachable and tasty, it's a wine worth seeking out if you're in the mood for a red and you don't want to unleash a monster from the cellar.

Mission Hill Family Estate Winery 1999 Reserve Merlot

Okanagan Valley $$ (553313)

The lighter style of this Merlot doesn't hinder the make-up of the wine. Attractive notes of cherry and blueberry with some floral fragrance point to a cooler vintage than 1998 and 2000. A soft palate accents the fruit flavours with a balanced acidity that helps to keep the firm tannins at bay. Finishes with a spicy flash. Drinking well now—but keep away from overly gamy meats.

Pelee Island Winery 2000 Vinedressers Merlot

Pelee Island $ (612622)

Produced from vines cultivated on the island, which just happens to be Canada's southernmost wine region, this wine has a lot of concentration. Chocolate notes with black cassis and vanilla. On the palate, a strong presence of oak with dark berry and chocolate flavours. Soft tannins with medium acidity combine to create a middleweight wine that would be a perfect match for lamb, duck and beef stews.

Peller Estates 1999 Andrew Peller Signature Series Merlot
Niagara Peninsula $$$$ (981142)
A deliciously attractive wine that sets the scene with wafts of cherry, cedar, vanilla and coffee. Rich cherry flavours abound on the palate with supple tannins and bright acidity providing the infrastructure to carry the wine through to a spicy finish. Decant and serve with funky cheese, red meats or with a good cigar after dinner.

Peller Estates 1999 Private Reserve Merlot
Niagara Peninsula $$ (981225)
A well-built wine that is both tasty and full of body, but it doesn't really come across as Merlot. It's more like a Cab Franc with black pepper and vanilla notes that carry over the palate. Soft tannins make for an attractive mouth-feel and a spicy finish cap this off-centred Merlot. Looking for a red to uncork at your next grilling party? This one would taste great and save you some cash.

Reif Estate Winery 2000 Merlot
Niagara Peninsula $$ (310914)
A little shy at first, this one opens up on the palate. Soft notes of earthy red berry fruits give way to intense fruit flavours of cassis and black-currant. A layer of oak rounds out the acidity and softens the firm tannins. A little youthful, this wine should be kept for a while or decanted for a few hours. Stir-fries with earthy veggies and grilled beef tenderloin would be an ideal match.

Sandhill 2000 Merlot
Okanagan Valley $$ (576751)
One of the signs of a great wine is the presence of perceived alcohol. When a wine begins to hit the fourteen per cent level, the threat of tasting the alcohol is very great. With this wine, wine-maker Howard Soon has managed to cloak the high alcohol with an abundance of concentrated fruit—mostly blackberry flavours. Coupled with a thin layer of oak, he has created a full-bodied wonder. Hugely extracted from a warmer-than-usual growing season, ripe fruit has been captured in the bottle. Big tannins with bright acidity point to a long life in the bottle. Best wait for a few years to unleash this monster. If you must indulge, please remember to decant.

Southbrook Winery 1999 Merlot
Lailey Vineyard
Niagara Peninsula $$$ (448365)
This single vineyard offering has lush notes of sweet cherry and blueberry. Toned tannins lift the intense flavours of vanilla and blueberry. Nicely integrated with a touch of sweetness from the oak, this wine has just the right amount of body to make it enjoyable now.

QUITE GOOD

Cave Spring Cellars 1999 Merlot
Niagara Peninsula $$$ (235051)
Showing a nice collection of extracted fruit, this wine has ample raspberry, plum and coffee aromas. The mouth-feel is on the lean side with some oak and herbaceous flavours mixing with the berry flavours. Short, tart finish leaves the wine hanging, but when paired with lamb, pork chops or roast beef, it should be able to hold its own.

Colio Estate Vineyards 1999 Merlot Reserve Barrel Aged CEV

Eire North Shore $$ (500447)

There's something to be said for getting down to basics with this simply styled Merlot. Although it spent a good year in the barrel, there's not a lot of oak lurking around. Subtle notes of cherry and cassis continue through the palate with a light mouth-feel. Drinking well now.

Hillebrand Estates 1997 Glenlake Vineyard Merlot Unfiltered

Niagara Peninsula $$$ (994574)

Showing its age, this offering has ample amounts of earthy barnyard notes. Sweet oak upfront leads to tobacco, leather and raspberry flavours. Rounded tannins are now fully integrated into the wine. Give it some time to breathe, and enjoy with rich, gamy meats.

Inniskillin Wines 1999 Schuele Vineyard Merlot

Niagara Peninsula $$ (586305)

This wine spent some serious downtime in oak. After the oak blows off, there's some elegant fruit on the palate. Plum and dark cherry with some tar flavours that linger through the finish. A big Merlot that needs more time to hit its stride.

Lailey Vineyard 2000 Merlot

Niagara Peninsula $$$

Looking for a funky red to go with your beef stew? Check this one out. Barnyard and charred oak with coconut milk. Soft on the palate with hints of black olive and vanilla, and a spicy touch on the finish. Lay this one down—or decant and dig in.

Lakeview Cellars 2000 Merlot
Butler's Grant Vineyard
Niagara Peninsula $$ (518068)
Built for the consumer who likes to drink youthful reds. Cherries abound in the glass, from the aromas to the flavours. A sweet oak touch enhances the flavours and gives the wine an added attraction.

Lakeview Cellars 2000 Reserve Merlot
Niagara Peninsula $$$ (565838)
A young wine that has emerging characters of raspberry and coffee. Layers of oak and fruit float around the tannins. Tight finish with a spicy touch adds complexity to the wine. Let this one integrate a bit more in the bottle.

Mission Hill Family Estate Winery 2000 Merlot
Okanagan Valley $$ (496109)
A lighter-style Merlot that would appeal to those who like their reds a little airy. Candied cherry flavours with medium tannins and a touch of vanilla. Drinking well now.

Peller Estates Okanagan 2000 Private Reserve
Barrel-Aged Merlot
Okanagan Valley $$ (618322)
Big, fruity red—at least on the nose. On the palate, it comes across as a lightweight Merlot with soft fruit and tight tannins. It's like riding a rollercoaster—up and down with a quick finish.

Quails' Gate Estate Winery 2000 Limited
Reserve Merlot
Okanagan Valley $ (446062)
Freshly bottled, this wine has the makings of a great wine. Streams of plum, dark cherry and cedar float out of the glass. Youthful tannins with a veil of smoky oak cloak the fruit. Racy and a bit tight, this limited offering should improve nicely over time.

Stoney Ridge Cellars 1999 Bench Merlot
Niagara Peninsula $ (544601)
A richly dense Merlot that combines ripe sweet
cherry and raspberry with a slight earthy angle.
Intense dark berry flavours with a core of acidity
and firm tannins that point to a lengthy life in the
bottle. Slightly aggressive, it's drinking well now
but could use a few more years to fully open up.

Strewn Wines 2000 Merlot Terroir
Niagara Peninsula $$ (618579)
Herbaceous characters of mint and cherry
blossoms. Redcurrant on the palate with some
smoky ash traits. Intense with tight tannins and
robust acidity, this wine leaves room to come
together more in the bottle. Let it sit around for
a little while.

Strewn Wines 1999 Merlot
Niagara Peninsula $ (467621)
Tart cherry and cassis flavours with a lot of tannins.
Creamy palate from a touch of sweet oak, it
has the weight and acidity to develop into a
table topper.

Thirty Bench Wines 1999 Merlot Reserve
Niagara Peninsula $$$$
This is one hot wine. High alcohol content knocks
the fruit around on the palate. Blueberry and
blackcurrant flavours manage to climb through
the heat. Spicy finish adds another notch to
this hottie.

Thomas and Vaughan Vintners 2000 Merlot Estate Reserve
Niagara Peninsula $$
Floral, mint and chocolate come drifting out of the
glass. Meaty and rich, there's a textured earthiness to the palate. Intense and extracted, the tannins are tight, but the flavours manage to
follow through to the finish. Shows great promise
after a few years.

Tinhorn Creek Vineyards 2000 Merlot
Okanagan Valley $$ (530725)
Give this one some time to integrate in the bottle. It's a shy wine that doesn't really express itself. Some buttery oak flavours with cherries lurk underneath. Although it started to open up after a while in the glass, the presence of firm tannins hindered further development. Let this one find itself before uncorking.

PINOT NOIR

Pinot Noir is the problem child of the vineyard. Call it the Robert Downey Jr. of the wine world because of its puzzling capacity for reaching the highest of highs and plumbing the lowest of lows. It is a complete enigma for growers and vintners alike who are desperate to know what makes Pinot tick. Often dubbed the Heartbreak Grape or referred to as winemaking's Holy Grail, this inconsistent grape variety is capable of producing the greatest wines in the world. But consumers have to kiss a lot of frogs before they meet a Pinot worthy of being crowned a prince.

From a winemaking perspective, Pinot demands a greater investment of time and money in the vineyard and at the winery, which is why none of the panel's recommended wines are what you would call cheap. For instance, Pinot Noir benefits from aging in new French oak, the most expensive wood barrels on the market.

FOOD PAIRING SUGGESTIONS
The most food-friendly of the red wine family, Pinot Noir is happy served with most things available at the butcher shop: pork loin or chops, lamb, veal, steak, chicken and game birds, including pheasant and duck. It also pairs nicely with salmon, tuna and snapper.

"Pinot Noir gets our best wood and most of our attention despite the fact it doesn't make us most of our money," explained Creekside Estate Winery winemaker Marcus Ansems, who puts his heart and soul into creating subtle and elegant Pinot Noir wines. "I love it and everyone in the cellar loves Pinot, too, so they stay the extra hours and put in the extra work.

"Pinot is twice as hard to grow, twice as fickle as any other grape," he continued. "It's one of those styles that you never get sick of because you never get it right."

Classic Pinot Noir characteristics are straw-berries, cherries, damp soil or compost, and barn-yard or horse stables. Newcomers should know that the gamy or rustic aromas are more pleasant than they might seem on first blush. But all Pinot discussions start and end with texture or mouth-feel. Great Pinot is round with a velvety supple-ness and a deep penetrating flavour.

The grape's native land is Burgundy in France, which shares some climatic conditions with both Niagara and British Columbia's cool-climate growing regions. Canadian vintners are starting to produce some amazing Pinot Noir, often only in small batches that are snapped up by a cult following. Both regions are working to establish a benchmark from which consistently good wine will flow. That work is starting to pay off, as taster Linda Bramble noted, "These wines show we don't have to take a back seat to anyone when it comes to Pinot."

Two wines stood head and shoulders above the other Pinot Noirs in our tasting. Both received five-star ratings, albeit for totally different reasons. Creekside has uncorked a classic Burgundy, while Peller's Okanagan winery delivers an attractive and approachable Pinot that's a fruit explosion for your taste buds.

Tasting Panel: MA, LB, WS, CW

VINES AWARD

Creekside Estate Winery 2000 Pinot Noir Marcus Ansems Signature Reserve

Niagara Peninsula $$$

A card-carrying Pinot Noir, this wine is more Burgundian than most bottles exported to this country from Pinot Noir's fatherland. The key characters—barnyard, cherries and chocolate—are fully developed. The red fruit takes a leading role, with a touch of sweetness and floral notes adding complexity. This is a big, intense wine that leaves you wanting more. It doesn't give an inch when compared with many $50-plus bottles from Burgundy, California or Oregon. This wine would make superb company for grilled steak or salmon, lamb or stews.

Peller Estates Okanagan 2000 Private Reserve Pinot Noir

Okanagan Valley $$ (618314)

A prime example of Pinot Noir's sexy, decadent side, Peller's wine has a dense, plush texture and is jam-packed with loads of slightly sweet fruit. All of that supple fruit is countered with good tannins and the focussing influence of vanilla and oak spice. Undeniably, there's freshness and powerful flavour. This wine could be served with a wide variety of foods, from mildly seasoned pasta dishes to grilled red meats.

HIGHLY RECOMMENDED

CedarCreek Estate Winery 2000
Platinum Reserve Pinot Noir
Okanagan Valley $$$ (585711)
Another fruity take on Pinot, this juicy, bright wine has a serious side thanks to a nice edge of spicy oak. The palate is lush and beautifully integrated, showcasing layers of ripe fruit and floral notes. Relatively dense and full of flavor, it's also soft, succulent and ready for immediate enjoyment. This is a delicious wine to savour as you decide when to throw the steaks on the barbecue or ponder some of life's bigger mysteries.

Creekside Estate Winery 2000 Pinot Noir
Niagara Peninsula $$ (572172)
An excellent choice for fans of earthier, classically styled Pinot Noir. This has the elusive smoky and slightly gamy intensity of the best bottles from Burgundy and the Rhône. Nice complex character, including a seductive violet note, and big standout fruit flavours. This wine offers amazing value for the price—a rarity in the world of Pinot Noir. Buy in quantity (three bottles or more) and enjoy over the next four years or so as the wine sweetens and harmonizes over the short term and develops more complexity with longer aging.

Creekside Estate Winery 1999
Marcus Ansems Signature Pinot
Niagara Peninsula $$$
The debut vintage of Creekside's reserve series establishes a signature style—savoury earth and spice character, with good intensity and concentrated fruit. Tasters remarked this wine is "very Burgundian" on account of its mushroom and barnyard notes and silky, elegant texture. It's a little bit country, a little bit Ritz Carlton: an impressive wine, with some dirt under its fingernails, but impeccable table manners. It's worth the splurge for a couple of bottles: one for now, one for holiday turkey down the road.

Inniskillin Wines 1999 Founders' Reserve Pinot Noir

Niagara Peninsula $$$ (558130)

This skillfully rendered wine knits together ripe, raisiny fruit with some barnyard funk and spicy oak flavours. The floral and meaty aromas recall prime Rhône wines, while the good, rich core of tender fruit speaks to the care and attention afforded this wine in the vineyard and winery. Drinking nicely now, it will develop over the next three to six years. This charming, robust wine is well suited for winter drinking with hearty stews and roasts.

RECOMMENDED

Inniskillin Okanagan Vineyards 1999 Pinot Noir Estate Bottled

Okanagan Valley $$ (530840)

Taste this wine and enjoy the classic Pinot Noir character that's often impossible to find at this price: supple texture, complex leather and cinnamon notes and a rich core of juicy cherry fruit. It's a great wine for business or casual entertaining as it has all of the hallmarks of an expensive Burgundy, including food compatibility.

Inniskillin Okanagan Vineyards 1998 Pinot Noir Estate Bottled

Okanagan Valley $$ (558437)

A wonderfully rich Pinot with layers of red fruit and oak notes, especially vanilla. A penetrating, well-made wine with deep, concentrated flavours, it is a triumph for the money. It should cellar well for five years or more, but it's quite charming now. Serve with robust red-meat dishes.

Inniskillin Wines 2000
Montague Estate Vineyard Pinot Noir
Niagara Peninsula $$ (586404)

A little introverted right now, this wine has all of the virtues that distinguish truly great Pinot: purity of fruit, typical earth and fruit aromas, velvety mouth-feel and balanced structure, with oak, body and tannin singing the same harmonious song. Enjoyable for the savoury-sweet note that lingers on the palate. Drink from 2003 to 2006.

Kacaba Vineyards 2000 Butler's Grant Vineyard Pinot Noir
Niagara Peninsula $$ (four-bottle box labelled Three Guys Pinot)

This fresh and flavourful Pinot displays interesting candied character, with nuances of anise, violets, gummy bears and tropical spices. It's even a bit sweet on the palate, but not so much that it would seem cloying or out of the question to serve with food. This decidedly unique wine would be a good match for cedarplank salmon or duck.

Lailey Vineyard 2000 Pinot Noir
Niagara Peninsula $$

This is an eye-opener. Lailey's Pinot shows how this unique grape can be light in body but pack a tremendous wallop. Imagine the thin geek from those Charles Atlas ads in old comic books knocking the tar out of the beefcake dude who dared kick sand in his face. It's smoky and meaty, with positive mixed berry flavours and a lush texture.

Marynissen Estates 2000 Pinot Noir
Butler's Grant Vineyard
Niagara Peninsula $$ (four-bottle box labelled Three Guys Pinot)

This single-vineyard Pinot offers intense black cherry and raspberry fruit and nuances of herbs,

earth, violets and vanilla. While it's ready to drink now, it has the structure and stuffing to develop over the long term. This wine makes an especially good match for hearty pasta dishes such as mushroom lasagna.

Mission Hill Family Estate Winery 2000 Pinot Noir Bin 99

Okanagan Valley $ (118844)

This charmer offers Pinot character with no discordant notes—a remarkable achievement at this price. The value-priced Bin 99 delivers generous ripe fruit, including the usual suspects of cherry and strawberry, along with rhubarb and grapefruit. This is fresh, clean and fruity—a solid choice for a wedding wine or group entertaining.

Mission Hill Family Estate Winery 2000 Reserve Pinot Noir

Okanagan Valley $$ (545012)

A fruit-driven Pinot Noir that does well in capturing the typical cherry and raspberry characteristics found in many warm-climate Pinots. Leaning on the lighter side, red berry fruits dominate the palate with a hint of herbaceous character. Balanced by a good dose of acidity, the fruit rolls from start through to a medium finish. Clean and well made, it's one to be enjoyed on its own or with lightly spiced meats, fish and pastas.

Quails' Gate Estate Winery 2000 Pinot Noir Limited Release

Okanagan Valley $$ (585760)

A good choice if you like dry fruity reds. This medium-bodied Pinot is a nice light red, driven by medicinal cherry and soft raspberry flavours. The texture is silky, the finish mild and soft. It's delicious by the glass and could pair up with a range of cheese and hors d'oeuvres.

Thornhaven Estates 2000 Pinot Noir

Okanagan Valley $ (730366)

The tantalizing licorice, chocolate and concentrated cherry aromas make for a sterling first impression, followed up nicely by the bright, pure fruit flavours on the palate. This simple but eminently quaffable wine pits a core of deep fruit flavours against a balancing edge of acidity. Enjoy with or without food.

Three Guys 2000 Pinot Noir
Butler's Grant Vineyard

Niagara Peninsula $$ (four-bottle box labelled Three Guys Pinot)

The fourth bottle of a special box of wine produced by the Three Guys: Marynissen's John Marynissen, Kacaba's Jim Warren and Lakeview's Eddy Gurinskas. The limited edition box of single-vineyard Pinot features one of each winemaker's bottlings and this blend of the Three Guys's wine. It's an intriguing wine, with aromatic licorice, chocolate, vanilla and oak spice notes. On the palate, there's candied cherry and floral notes, which sound sweeter than they taste. Its supple but lively texture was a hit with the panelists.

Tinhorn Creek Vineyards 2000 Pinot Noir

Okanagan Valley $ (530709)

An excellent pouring Pinot, with ripe strawberry and cherry fruit, soft acidity and a plush mouth-feel. It doesn't scream Pinot Noir, but that fruit certainly does a lot of talking. Buy by the case and enjoy as your house wine over the next year. This wine has all the drinkability of a velvety Merlot, but retains the versatility of Pinot. It will complement a wide variety of food and could even be chilled down slightly to increase its quaffing quotient for barbecue season.

QUITE GOOD

EastDell Estates Winery 2000 Pinot Noir Novello Vineyard

Niagara Peninsula $

Black pepper tickles the nose and supple fruit tweaks the taste buds in this straight-up wine. It's interesting and a little introverted. Good colour, flavour and body.

Henry of Pelham Family Estates Winery 1999 Pinot Noir

Niagara Peninsula $$ (268391)

An intense, opulent style of Pinot, which one taster described as smelling like "a gym bag after a win." Smoke, earth and cherry and currant fruit are part of the package, which all tasters agreed was truly Burgundian in nature. Enjoy with mushroom or truffle dishes, ratatouille, duck or roast venison.

Inniskillin Wines 2000 Pinot Noir

Niagara Peninsula $ (261099)

This straightforward red wine won't dazzle you with its complexity, but it's off the charts in terms of enjoyment. It's chunky with cherry and beetroot notes. Serve with hamburgers, pizza, pasta and grilled meat—anything that will stand up to a flavourful red.

Jackson-Triggs Niagara Estate 2000 Proprietors' Reserve Pinot Noir

Niagara Peninsula $ (618405)

Beefy and big-boned, this Pinot is an interesting, well-made wine with smoky bacon, dried herbs and some stemmy notes. A lot of complex notes help dress up this value-priced wine.

Konzelmann Estate Winery 1999 Pinot Noir
Niagara Peninsula $ (200584)
Soft berry flavours and silky texture are featured in this wine, which offers all of the crowd-pleasing smoothness of Pinot without any of the barnyard funk that sours some consumers. A little bit medicinal, a lot like Merlot, this is a go-to party wine.

Konzelmann Estate Winery 1998 Pinot Noir Reserve Unfiltered
Niagara Peninsula $$ (463141)
The aromas are muted, even after some time in the glass, but this introverted wine comes alive on the palate. Big red fruit flavours unwind along with layers of leather and oak. This wine will be a winner in a few years.

Pelee Island Winery 2000 Pinot Noir
Ontario $
A consistently good red wine that makes the most of its earthy fruit and spice flavours. The palate is a bit too candied to bring to the table, but your deck furniture will enjoy its simplistic charms.

Peller Estates 2000 Private Reserve Pinot Noir
Niagara Peninsula $$ (981282)
This rich, evocative red wine possesses an oaky nose with raspberry fruit and strong earthy character. It's not an overly complex wine, but an easy style that has some tannin to add backbone and some elegant features. All in all, this is a fairly intense, pleasantly ripe Pinot with a good structure and concentration.

Reif Estate Winery 2000 Pinot Noir
Niagara Peninsula $
As with the folk-pop of Badly Drawn Boy, the in-crowd is going to be all over this interesting, integrated Pinot Noir. Made in a light, very drinkable style, it pits pure fruit flavours against some offbeat, but enjoyable herbal notes. Dance bars ought to stock this beauty by the glass.

Stoney Ridge Cellars 1999 Bench Pinot Noir
Niagara Peninsula $ (240903)
Here's a nice value-priced Pinot with good concentration and expressive cherry and raspberry
flavours. Some nice toasty oak notes mellow its
deep fruit flavours.

Sumac Ridge Estate Winery 1999 Pinot Noir
Okanagan Valley $ (392415)
Pleasant black cherry and floral aromas are the
most beguiling features of this straightforward
red wine. It has nice flavours and an appealing
mouth-feel that will delight with its abundance of
juicy fruit.

OTHER RED WINES

Gamay Noir

If you've ever had a Beaujolais red wine, then you've had a Gamay Noir. Made popular by wine-makers of Beaujolais, France, Gamay has become a transition wine for wine enthusiasts. For many novice wine consumers their journey of wine appreciation starts with light, fruity white wines and evolves towards the more complex and full-bodied reds. To get from A to B would be a challenge if it were not for Gamay Noir.

Typically, Gamay is built as an expressively fruity, light-bodied red wine with low tannins and high acidity. The approachable style places the wine between the gentle features of whites and the robust, bold features of reds. Since it is usually best enjoyed in its youth, Gamay also gives many

FOOD PAIRING SUGGESTIONS
Most Gamay Noirs are built to be consumed now. The fruity, light-bodied styles would go well with hamburgers and tofu burgers. Grilled chicken and pork and tossed salads would also make for good companions. Some of the bolder Gamay wines being built in Canada could stand up to gourmet pizzas and hot chicken wings. Perhaps the ideal setting would be an evening of Hockey Night in Canada with take-out pizza and hot wings.

wine lovers a chance to try a red wine without having to wait for it to mature for five years or spend the big bucks on an aged red, although some Gamay's have been known to age elegantly for more than five to ten years.

The fact that many Gamays are built to be unleashed early and often has also given rise to yearly celebrations under the banner of Beaujolais Nouveau or Gamay Nouveau. It's a fitting celebration as the Gamay is usually the first red vintage wine every year.

In Canada, Gamay has found a home in Ontario, although there are a couple of producers in British Columbia trying to get it to catch on. Like the Pinot Noir grape, the Gamay thrives in the cool-climate wine regions of Niagara and the northern Okanagan Valley. A vigorous varietal, the grape consistently reaches its full potential year after year. Although not widely produced by wineries in Canada, those that do produce the friendly red wine are beginning to emerge from the shadow cast by the Beaujolais giants. If you want a taste test, buy a Gamay from the list below and pair it with similarly priced Beaujolais—and you be the judge as to who makes the better Gamay.

Tasting Panel: TK , RP, WS, CW

VINES AWARD

Thirteenth Street Wine Co. 1999 Sandstone Gamay

Niagara Peninsula $$

A lot of the French Beaujolais is like bubble gum pop music—all flash and no substance. This complex Gamay is more suited to those with an ear for Billie Holiday. Huge notes of blueberry and plum with toasty vanilla offer an attractive entrance to the wine. The layers in the glass are deep, rich and full of flavour. A seductive sweet touch on the front gives way to rolling soft tannins that lift up the ripe plum and dark berry flavours. A voluptuous wine that will age gracefully. A perfect match with gamy meats such as venison and caribou.

HIGHLY RECOMMENDED

Cave Spring Cellars 2000 Reserve Gamay

Niagara Peninsula $$ (289082)

Another stellar Gamay from Cave Spring. The success of this wine comes from its balance. Some wines impress on the opening, or have a great mid palate or finish with a bang, but to be great, a wine needs to carry itself from start to finish. This one does just that as notes of cherry and plum with an undercurrent of earthiness give way to more concentrated fruit on the palate. Deep layers of black spice, cherry and blackberry are enhanced by firm tannins and balanced acidity on the palate. A lingering spicy finish caps off this reserve. Built for food, this would be an ideal match for red meat dishes or fall-harvested vegetables.

Colio Estate Vineyards 2000 Gamay Noir CEV

Lake Erie North Shore $ (342451)

When you see "barrel aged" on the label, you know you're not getting a light red. This Gamay is full of toasty oak with generous flavours of ripe, dusty cherry. It's like walking through a cherry orchard in mid July with a lingering fragrance of smouldering pruned wood from a farm field. A touch of sweetness on the front gives way to lively raspberry and cherry flavours. Integrated tannins make the wine enjoyable now, but a few years in the bottle could give it even more depth. Match with grilled mushrooms and roasts.

RECOMMENDED

Château des Charmes Winery 2000 Gamay Noir

Niagara Peninsula $ (057349)

A "meaty" wine is how one panelist described this big red. There are plums, cherries and black-currants with a touch of earthiness on the nose. These characteristics carry over to the palate with solid tannins propping up the flavours through to a very spicy finish. If you're ravenous for some big meats, wash it all down with this Gamay.

Henry of Pelham Family Estate Winery 2000 Gamay

Niagara Peninsula $ (291112)

A finely balanced wine that manages to hang onto the fruit while spending a little downtime in the barrel. Enticing aromas of vanilla bean, black-currant and white pepper segue into a medium-bodied wine that is both rich and refreshing. A good expression of the grape, there's enough weight to carry the wine through to a spicy finish. Try with penne pasta with tomatoes or oven-baked curry-spiced chicken.

Hillebrand Estates 2000 Harvest Gamay
Niagara Peninsula $ (291732)
This Gamay never saw the inside of a barrel. Built in the traditional Gamay style, there's much more bright fruit in this red. Tasty flavours of strawberry, redcurrant and cranberry wash over the palate with a streak of acidity that gives the wine a fresh feeling. A racy finish makes it a great match for gourmet pizza or spicy hot wings.

Maleta Vineyards 2000 Gamay Noir Reserve
Niagara Peninsula $$

Although it came across as a Pinot Noir to some panelists, this reserve has all the markings of a gentle touch. Cedar, pepper and plum show this wine spent some downtime (but not too much) in wood. On the palate, the fruit is more expressive, with a thin line of cedar providing a pleasant respite from the fruit. Elegant, yet bold enough to be paired with rich, red meats or spicy dishes.

Peller Estates 2000 Vineyard Series Gamay Noir
Niagara Peninsula $ (981431)
First impression is a little youthful with herbaceous notes, but after lingering in the glass a bit, vanilla, currant and pepper begin to peek out. A dash of sweetness gives way to smoky flavours, with plum and currant adding some substance to all the oak. Length and balance are the keys to this recommended wine—along with the great value. Order in pizza and pull the cork on this one.

QUITE GOOD

Cave Spring Cellars 2000 Gamay
Niagara Peninsula $ (228569)
A youthful offering that could use some time to develop. Chokecherry and a smouldering oak nuance dominate from the nose to the finish. Although it evolved more in the glass over time, there's a lot of smoky oak that needs to find its way through the wine. Your best bet would be to decant and serve with baby back ribs.

Château des Charmes Winery 2000 Gamay Noir Droit
Niagara Peninsula $ (582353)
A simple Gamay that has the weight and acidity to match heavier meats, but the firm tannins need some time to relax. It's like a tightly wound dog that's been kept on a leash all day. Once it's loose, it's all over the place. Give this one some time to calm down and it should be a fine companion.

Domaine Combret 2000 Gamay Saint Vincent Private Reserve
Okanagan Valley $$$ 624585)
This lightweight Gamay is drinking well now. Strawberry, raspberry and black pepper capture the essence of the wine. Higher acids compete with the tannins for space on the palate, but the fruit manages to hold together through the finish. Spaghetti and meatballs would be reason enough to open this one.

Peller Estates 2000 Private Reserve Gamay Noir
Niagara Peninsula $$ (981241)
Drinking very well now, this wine is designed to be enjoyed within the next year. Ripe cherries and spice flavours are balanced by a nice streak of acidity that lifts the fruit through the tannins and to the finish. If you're looking for a mid week wine to kick back and relax with, give this one a try with some blue cheese and crackers.

Syrah/Shiraz

The French call it Syrah, the Australians Shiraz, and in Canada, wine producers call it both. Talk about confusing. Although the Aussies have made Shiraz wildly popular, it's not a widely planted variety around the world. In France, Syrah is grown primarily in the northern Rhône, which produces elegant, yet complex wines that display cassis and blackcurrant flavours with great aging potential. In Australia Shiraz, which is Syrah that was brought to the country back in the mid 1800s, is mostly grown in the warmer climate of Southern Australia. Aussie Shiraz is typically black ink in colour with intense flavours of plum, leather and black pepper with huge tannins. If it's made properly, and you're willing to pay the price, an Australian Shiraz can last for years.

With the arrival of Australian and French winemakers to wineries in Canada over the past few years, there has been some experimentation with Syrah plantings. This year, eight wines were submitted to the tasting, and by all accounts, the numbers will double within the next year. But, why plant more varietals when most wineries are already producing too many different wines? "There's such demand for fuller-bodied reds that Syrah, like Merlot, also a relatively earlier-ripening grape, has a potential to be a more consistent red varietal," explained Thomas Pennachetti of Cave Spring Cellars in Jordan. Judging from the tasting, Syrah has great potential—but only time will tell if consumers will be willing to switch from Rhône Syrah and Aussie Shiraz.
Tasting Panel: TK, RP, WS, CW

FOOD PAIRING SUGGESTIONS
Gamy, rich meat stews, root vegetable stews, hearty mushroom soups, roasted pork loin in black pepper and mustard. The ideal setting for Shiraz is the last barbecue of the season with a CFL game playing in the background, and the leaves turning vibrant shades of red and orange.

HIGHLY RECOMMENDED

Cave Spring Cellars 2000 Syrah
Niagara Peninsula $$

Built like a Rhône Syrah, this has a textbook earthy note with sweaty leather, plum and spices. A long growing season in 2000 allowed the fruit to ripen and it shows with the huge extraction in this wine. Dense blackberry fruit with black pepper is heightened by a robust acidity and medium tannins. It's not an in-your-face red, but why buy something that's all sizzle when you can get substance? It's like listening to Radiohead instead of Nickelback. Try with peppercorn steak.

Jackson-Triggs Okanagan Estate 2000 Shiraz Proprietors' Reserve
Okanagan Valley $$ (593103)

Aussie-born winemaker Bruce Nicholson has managed to create a Shiraz ringer that wouldn't be out of place in an Australian wine tasting. Like a boisterous fan at a hockey game, this wine stands out. Intense notes of jammy plum with tobacco and blackcurrant are the first none-too-subtle clues that this wine is huge. A monster in the mouth, it's packed full of black pepper and vanilla along with the dark berries. A touch of oaky sweetness gives this beast a gentle side, but its big weight and firm tannins scream through to the finish. A great wine for a hearty meal such as stew.

Peninsula Ridge Estates Winery 2000 Syrah
Niagara Peninsula $$$$

Hire a French winemaker and you'll get French wine. At least with this Syrah that rule of thumb holds true. Peninsula Ridge's French winemaker Jean-Pierre Colas has managed to craft an earthy Syrah with bumbleberry notes. Dark berry flavours burst out of the palate with a touch of sweet oak in the front. Firm tannins lift the wine through to a spicy finish. Idea: buy, put in cellar and forget about it for a few years. Heck, if the wineries are willing to experiment with this grape, why don't you?

RECOMMENDED

Inniskillin Wines 2000 Brae Burn Estate Shiraz

Niagara Peninsula $$ (591479)

Inniskillin's Aussie winemaker Phillip Dowell brought his fondness for Shiraz to Canada when he arrived a few years ago. His 1999 debut Shiraz was a very limited offering, marking the twenty-fifth anniversary of Inniskillin. Although the 1999s were tough to track down, the 2000s should placate the palates of many Shiraz fans. Jam-packed with blueberry and blackberry with an attractive hint of cocoa, there's a lot going on. Finely balanced with medium tannins and nice lines of acidity, it finishes with a burst of spices.

Mission Hill Family Estate Winery 1999 Shiraz Reserve

Okanagan Valley $$ (585778)

This reserve straddles the fence between a big Shiraz and a complex Syrah. A subtle nose of cherry and rose petal notes with a dash of pepper gives way to more intense flavours and structure on the palate. A sweet touch upfront leads to more plum and spice flavours. This medium-bodied red has just enough tannins to carry the wine to the finish. It's drinking very well now, and would be a great match for tomato-based pasta dishes and spiced sausages.

Mission Hill Family Estate Winery 1999 Syrah Estate

Okanagan Valley $$$ (556332)

Talk about confusion—a Shiraz and Syrah from the same winery. A rare offering from Mission Hill, this Syrah has only been aged in French oak, unlike the Shiraz which spent time in both Yankee and French barrels. An elegant red with lighter notes of cassis and redcurrants. Upfront fruit intensity gives way to a soft cocoa finish that makes for a very attractive wine. Match with salmon steaks over a bed of steamed rice with roasted vegetables.

Red Hybrids

BACO NOIR

If Bob and Doug McKenzie were wine drinkers, they would probably uncork a few bottles of Baco Noir while watching *Hockey Night in Canada*. It's a hearty hybrid that grows very well in Canada's cooler wine regions. Although not widely planted in British Columbia, the robust red has been taken on by a few producers in Ontario and turned into a cult favourite. It's like the John Candy of the wine world—big, boisterous, unpretentious and fun to be around.

Cultivation and consumption of Baco Noir (Baco, to friends) is to be encouraged. The French hybrid is in no way the future of Canada's winemaking industry, but it offers a decidedly different wine to Cabernet. "Baco gets that plush fruit character, that's what makes it interesting. And, as it ages, cigar and cedary notes develop, which add to its enjoyment," says Matthew Speck, vice-president of viticulture at Henry of Pelham Family Estate Winery in St. Catharines. Henry of Pelham helped elevate the lowly grape variety into a vineyard star simply by giving it the same care and attention afforded to European divas, vinifera varieties such as Pinot Noir and Merlot. As a character in George Bernard Shaw's *Fanny's First Play* states, "No one is a king who isn't treated like one."

Proof of Baco, and other hybrid vines, second-class nature comes from VQA legislation stipulating that even if the grapes are produced from a single, estate vineyard in Niagara, the label must carry the generic Ontario appellation. Unfortunately that doesn't help consumers separate serious and refined Bacos from the thin, acidic versions commonly produced by less thoughtful vintners.

Speck says the key to producing lush and luscious red wine from Baco comes from reducing

FOOD PAIRING SUGGESTIONS
Quintessentially Canadian, Baco is best enjoyed with caribou, venison, duck and even back bacon over the grill at the cottage. The best examples are also fully flavoured enough to make for easy-drinking sipping wines, ideally enjoyed in the fall and winter.

the crop down to one bunch per shoot. (The vine, he explains, generally produces up to four per shoot.) Less fruit means more sun and nutrients for the remaining grapes. Better grapes, better wine, it's that simple. In the winery, the fruit for the reserve Baco continues to receive the five-star treatment, hibernating for up to two years in new American oak barrels. A portion of Merlot is added to the finished wine to help the structure and round out the palate.

Tasting Panel: FG, WS, MS, CW

VINES AWARD

Henry of Pelham Family Estate Winery 2000 Baco Noir Reserve

Ontario $$ (461699)

The reigning king of Baco Noir, Henry of Pelham has established the benchmark for wonderfully tasty and robust wines from this second-class citizen of the vineyard. This vintage is one of Henry of Pelham's best reserve bottlings to date. Dark chocolate and plummy, rich fruit flavours partner with hints of tobacco and coconut. The weight and intensity of this wine stains your tongue a deep purple and leaves your taste buds wanting more. Deep and delicious, the finish is long and flavourful. Drink over the next five or six years.

HIGHLY RECOMMENDED

Birchwood Estate Wines 2000 Baco Noir

Ontario $

A seriously good Baco from Beamsville, Ontario, Birchwood's 2000 has plummy fruit, pepper, tobacco and leather aromas. The medium-bodied wine continues to impress on the palate, where ripe dark fruit and other rich flavours compete for attention. Its bright acidity and tasty profile will make it a dinner-table favourite when barbecued steak or venison sausage are on offer.

RECOMMENDED

Henry of Pelham Family Estate Winery 2001 Baco Noir

Ontario $ (270926)

A piquant cinnamon aroma adds some excitement to the medley of ripe red fruit found on the nose. The wine is round, but a little lean, with a bright acidity that would work well with a variety of rustic dishes. This is ready to be uncorked now.

Lakeview Cellars 2000 Baco Noir

Ontario $ (307181)

Subtle berry aromas and a touch of bacon and cedar on the nose make for a slightly reserved first impression. But the wine's personality unfolds quickly, with a rich, silkiness to the palate that invigorates the taste buds. Smooth and well balanced, with generous fruit, this is an easy drinking Baco that will be the life of any party. Break out some old mixed tapes (alright, the Cult) and uncork this charmer.

Pelee Island Winery 2000 Baco Noir

Ontario $ (485128)

You really can't tell a wine by its label. If you're familiar with the Pelee Island labels with their use of indigenous animals and plants, you probably order your wine by the item on the bottle, instead of the name of the wine. It's a good marketing ploy to get you to remember the wine, but in the case of Baco Noir, the Hibiscus flower on the label doesn't really match what's inside. It's definitely not a floral wine. More like big and meaty with robust flavours of plum and black-currant. Rounded tannins with a balanced acidity combine to produce a full-bodied red. Every year, Pelee Island manages to produce a wonderful Baco at a great price and 2000 keeps the streak alive. Enjoy with homemade hamburgers or hearty stews.

QUITE GOOD

Ancient Coast 2000 Baco Noir
Ontario $ (559138)
Raspberry and vanilla are the value-added flavours for this Baco, which features a fleshy core of fruit that runs more to the tart/sour cherry and currant spectrum. A little lean, a little green, this is best enjoyed with a meal.

Grape Tree Estate Wines 2000 Baco Noir
Ontario $
Rounder, softer take on Baco, with pleasant cinnamon scent and slight fishy nose. Well-integrated plum and oak flavours, with a lingering finish. A chunky fruit charmer best enjoyed by the glass or with casual meals, such as pizza and wings.

Harrow Estates 2000 Baco Noir
Ontario $ (559179)
This light-bodied wine is unassuming and ready to be enjoyed. Some stalky notes mingle with richer currant flavours on the nose and palate. Chill slightly and enjoy with simple pasta and tomato sauce or veal Parmesan.

MARÉCHAL FOCH

Another French hybrid cultivated by a handful of die-hards, Maréchal Foch sounds like the name of a French-Canadian hockey player: "Maréchal Foch, Montreal's leading scorer, rushes down the left wing. He shoots, he ..." You get the idea. This is a winter-hardy vine, and winemakers can count on the grapes reaching their full potential year after year. Although not widely popular with wine aficionados, it has its loyal followers. There are a few wineries in Ontario and British Columbia making Maréchal Foch, but wineries in Quebec have planted acre upon acre of the varietal.
Tasting Panel: FG, WS, MS, CW

FOOD PAIRING SUGGESTIONS
Mushroom-based dishes and gamy meats such as venison, rabbit and duck.

VINES AWARD

Malivoire Wine Co. 2000 Old Vines Foch
Ontario $$ (551036)
Two panelists summed this knockout with one word—beautiful. Malivoire's Old Vines Foch has all the drama of *Cinderella*: lowly servant girl is whisked to the ball where she intoxicates Prince Charming. Lowly Foch gets dressed up in the winemaking finery generally reserved for Cabernet or Pinot—be still our hearts. Intense aromas and flavours, including smoked meat, bacon and leather notes, hang in the background of a beautiful full, lush palate. Although drinking well now, a few more years toiling in the cellar will give this wine even more regal powers.

HIGHLY RECOMMENDED

Thomas and Vaughan Vintners 2000 Maréchal Foch
Ontario $
A smoky, sweetish palate makes for a crowd-pleasing red wine that can be called into service for family dinners and other potentially awkward entertaining situations. This is a nice smooth wine that will delight Sister Suzy, Brother John, Cousin Michael, Auntie Gin and the like. Enjoy with or without food, even without relatives, over the next two to four years.

RECOMMENDED

Thomas and Vaughan Vintners 2001 Maréchal Foch
Ontario $
The Spice Girl that never was: Tasty Spice. For wine consumers who want (really, really want) a full-bodied red with rich fruit and funky meat flavours. More than a one-hit wonder, this wine has enough ripe fruit character and intensity to warrant buying in quantity to enjoy over the coming months and years. Drink now to 2005.

QUITE GOOD

Harrow Estates 2000 Maréchal Foch
Ontario $ (277459)
Light fruity nose and palate make for a good, gluggable wine that will add a spark of excitement to Friday pizza night or mid week chicken and salad dinners. Nice intensity of fruit and a decent finish.

Hernder Estate Winery 1999 Foch
Ontario $ (557371)
Fine astringency and ripe core of fruit brighten up this mellow model of Foch. Plain and simple (not that's there's anything wrong with that), this wine would be happiest resting on the coffee table beside the pizza box watching the Leafs square off against Ottawa or the Raptors take on the Knicks.

St. Hubertus Estate Winery 2000 Oak Bay Vineyard Maréchal Foch
British Columbia $
Rich and jammy red, this is a smooth, easy-drinking red. Nicely polished fruit flavours linger. Enjoy over the next couple of years by the glass or at the dinner table.

DESSERT WINE

ICEWINE

Icewine. The sweet nectar of the gods. The golden honey of wine. Whatever you want to call it, Icewine is sweet, seductive and expensive. It's a rare and elegant wine unlike any other. It's made from frozen grapes that have been left on the vine for late harvest, usually in December and January. According to Canadian Icewine standards set by the VQA, Icewine grapes can only be harvested after the temperature reaches -8°C or colder. The grapes are pressed immediately while still frozen. Such grapes yield only 75 to 100 litres of intensely flavoured juice per tonne of grapes. The result is a higher-priced wine due to this vastly reduced volume of juice.

To craft an exquisite Icewine, the winemaker must balance the highly concentrated sugar

levels with the low acidity of the juice. An Icewine without balanced acidity is pancake syrup. Well-made vintages are sweet, but never cloying. With each passing vintage, winemakers are hitting the balanced mark on an increasingly regular basis.

Through a number of international wine competitions, including the prestigious VinExpo in France and VinItaly in Italy, Canadian Icewine has helped place Canadian wines on the world stage. The two most popular grapes for Canadian Icewine are Riesling and Vidal. In Ontario, the hardy Vidal grape was the first to be successfully turned into Icewine. Its thick skin makes it ideal for allowing the grape juice to freeze without splitting open and losing valuable liquid. Vidal is not as abundant in British Columbia, and Riesling has become a popular alternative in the Icewine arena. In both Ontario and British Columbia, many producers are crafting dazzling Riesling Icewines.

As the popularity of Icewine grows around the world, winemakers are continuing to experiment with different varieties in the hopes of creating more rare and exotic vintages. Gewürztraminer, Pinot Gris, Pinot Blanc, Ehrenfelser and red viniferas such as Cabernet Franc, Pinot Noir and Merlot all made appearances in our exhaustive tasting.

The fruit for the 2000 vintage in both British Columbia and Ontario was picked in ideal conditions in late December. "We finished picking before New Year's Eve. It was the first time in a while that I was able to enjoy ringing in the New Year without having to look at the thermometer," said Klaus Reif, proprietor and winemaker of Reif Estate Winery in Niagara-on-the-Lake. "We managed to pull in fruit with brix [natural grape sugar] in the mid-to-high 40s. We knew it was going to be a special vintage." The result has been some beautiful wines.

As for the aging capabilities of Icewine, the jury is still out, but generally, if the winemaker carefully

crafts the wine and hits the balance mark, Icewines can still be works of art after ten years in the cellar. One quick note: unless otherwise specified, the prices quoted are for the traditional 375 ml bottle. **Tasting Panel**: RC, SGB, WS, IS, CW

Vidal Icewine

VINES AWARD

Reif Estate Winery 2000 Vidal Icewine
Niagara Peninsula $$$$ (544775)
One of Canada's most consistent producers of awarding-winning Vidal Icewine, Reif Estate Winery has garnered a collection of international awards. The 2000 offering looks to continue the tradition, as it's a true benchmark Icewine. Enticing notes of toffee and caramel, with peach and apricot, awaken the senses. Once in the mouth, its lush texture washes the blend of fruit and caramel over the palate towards a long finish. Finely crafted and balanced, it's how a Vidal Icewine should be designed. Built with attention to detail, this is a showpiece wine that will impress even the most hardened Icewine critic.

HIGHLY RECOMMENDED

Lakeview Cellars 2000 Vidal Icewine
Niagara Peninsula $$/200ml (525672)
A close runner-up for the *Vines* Award, Lakeview's is a delightful treat for those looking for a bigger-bodied Icewine. Attractive characters of toffee, caramel and apricots are lifted on the palate by a streak of acidity, with the sugar amplifying the flavours by giving it some weight. Its fully developed body makes this an Icewine to be enjoyed on its own after dinner. Save the cake for another time.

Magnotta Wines 2000 Vidal Icewine
Merritt Road Vineyard
Niagara Peninsula $$$

Notes of dried apple, brown sugar and caramel give way to a bright, fruity explosion on the palate. Lush and flavourful, there's plenty of weight to make this an enjoyable sipper after dinner without the extra calories of dessert.

Pillitteri Estates Winery 2001 Vidal Icewine
Niagara Peninsula $$$$ (370007)

Bright fruit, crisp taste—that's the best way to describe this delicious Icewine. Freshly sliced pineapple and peach aromas. The fruit explodes across the palate with a streak of acidity thrusting the wine to a fine finish. Lighter in style, this classic would appeal to those who like their Icewine with a touch of elegance.

Reif Estate Winery 1999 Vidal Icewine
Niagara Peninsula $$$$ (544775)

This Icewine has taken top honours at a number of European wine competitions since it was released and it continues to show well. Elegant aromas of peach and lemon point to a lighter-styled Icewine. Indeed, on the palate it has a racy intensity that enhances the fruit flavours. An interesting spicy texture on the finish brings it full circle, leaving your palate looking for another sip.

Vineland Estates Winery 1999 Vidal Icewine
Niagara Peninsula $$$$

A wonderful wine that has all the key ingredients of a well-made Icewine. The shopping list includes caramel, toffee and apricot, with balanced acidity and sugar giving it a full-bodied texture. A unique oily texture on the finish adds to its great appeal.

RECOMMENDED

Château des Charmes Winery 1998 Vidal Icewine
Niagara Peninsula $$$$ (413732)
A wine that has received its fair share of trophies over the years, it's not showing signs of getting old and tired. Ripe apricots with golden honey best capture the essence of this wine. Mellower on the palate, the fruit is still lush and supple. It has enough weight to age for a few more years. Drinking extremely well now, but it could still stand some time in the cellar. A very well-made wine, worthy of its past awards.

EastDell Estates Winery 1999 Vidal Icewine
Niagara Peninsula $$$$
If you were looking for a subtle Icewine that doesn't overpower the senses, this would be one to search out. Plenty of citrus fruit flavours with hints of toffee. More racy in style, it's a crisp offering that is intense but quick on the finish. All the more reason to take another sip.

Inniskillin Wines 2000 Vidal Icewine
Niagara Peninsula $$$$ (591883)
If you want to have sweet dreams, why not cap your evening off with a sip of Icewine? This would be a perfect tonic for sleepless nights. Lemon and peach with a touch of toffee are the calling cards for this wine. A little on the sweet side, there's enough acidity to hold the wine together. You'll be sure to have sweet dreams after a glass of this one.

Konzelmann Estate Winery 2000 Vidal Icewine
Niagara Peninsula $$$$ (476192)

It's like dripping honey over a bowl of peaches and pineapples. With a lighter build dominated by the fruit, this Icewine has a lot of acidity, making it quite crisp. Some extra weight on the finish rounds a wine that could use some time to open up. An interesting creamy texture on the finish adds an interesting touch.

Mission Hill Family Estate Winery 1998 Reserve Vidal Icewine
Okanagan Valley $$$$ (532838)

The deep golden colour is the first sign you've entered aged Icewine territory. The second is the intense aromas of caramel, peach and even a hint of mint. On the palate, it has a lively acidity enhancing the caramel and peach flavours. Leaning on the light side, it's a delicious wine that should be enjoyed on its own.

Peninsula Ridge Estates Winery 2000 Vidal Icewine
Niagara Peninsula $$$$

Built like a layered fruitcake, this one has peach, mango and apricot, with a dollop of honey. On the palate, there's also a touch of burnt caramel. At its very core, it's well built with enough of the key parts to keep you coming back. It's deep, rich and textured, so cut back on dessert and save room for a glass of this one.

Southbrook Winery 2000 Vidal Icewine
Niagara Peninsula $$$ (525634)

If you've got a craving for something sweet, uncork this offering. Intense ripe apricot with peach and raisin characteristics are on display throughout the wine. A rum-like quality hits the mid palate with a heavy cloying coating carrying the fruit to the finish.

Stonechurch Vineyards 1999 Vidal Icewine

Niagara Peninsula $$$$ (477596)

Although this wine doesn't come across as Vidal Icewine, it still deserves high marks for tastiness. Interesting lily fragrance with some ginger spice and apricot notes. Intense flavours of anise and spice converge on the palate with a layer of acidity that helps to prop up the wine to its spicy finish.

QUITE GOOD

Hillebrand Estates 1999 Trius Vidal Icewine

Niagara Peninsula $$$$ (137687)

A quiet offering that has hints of peach and honey. A spark of energy livens up the wine on the palate, but it doesn't have the staying power. Still, an attractive wine to uncork as a special treat to yourself after a long day at the office.

Jackson-Triggs Niagara Estate 2000 Vidal Icewine Proprietors' Reserve

Niagara Peninsula $$$$ (594010)

It's like walking through a peach orchard with a beehive in the next field. Built on the light side, this Icewine has enough late-summer orchard fruit to make it a tasty treat, but not enough body to make it last. Ends with a nice toffee touch.

Stoney Ridge Cellars 1999 Vidal Icewine

Niagara Peninsula $$$$ (314682)

Showing hints of aging at a good clip, this one has sun-dried raisin with some honey and apricot notes still lurking around. On the palate, it's more of the same, with Madeira-like characters starting to push through. An interesting nutty finish rounds out a wine that should be consumed within the next year.

Thomas and Vaughan Vintners 2000 Vidal Icewine

Niagara Peninsula $$$

This wine is all about toffee. From the opening notes of toffee with a hint of caramel to its quick finish, this is a toffee-lover's dream. If you like chewy toffee put a bow around this one and give yourself a treat.

Willow Heights Winery 1999 Vidal Icewine

Niagara Peninsula $$$$ (453753)

Best described as a shy wine. Subtle characteristics of brown sugar and caramel provide the backdrop for a Vidal Icewine, but it's a lightweight that doesn't go the distance.

Riesling Icewine

VINES AWARD

Inniskillin Okanagan Vineyards 2000 Riesling Icewine Dark Horse Estate Vineyard

Okanagan Valley $$$$ (558445)

Definitely a dark horse in this field, as most Riesling Icewine comes from Niagara. An early cold snap in the Valley in 2000 allowed Icewine grapes to be harvested in near-perfect conditions, retaining intensity of flavours and concentrated brix. Typical lemon and peach blossom notes with an interesting subtext of caramel and toffee aromas. A heavier-styled Icewine, with an acidity that captures its success. Bright acids allow the wine to be slightly weighty without becoming cloying. Flavours of lemon, peach and pineapple dance over the palate and come to an elegant but crisp finish. A gem of an Icewine.

HIGHLY RECOMMENDED

Jackson-Triggs Niagara Estate 2000 Proprietors' Grand Reserve Riesling Icewine

Niagara Peninsula $$$$ (593970)

A wine that is best compared to the music of Diana Krall—both being elegant, soft and sexy. Concentrated notes of lemon, pineapple and honey give way to a lighter wine that balances its acid and sugar. Supple flavours of tropical fruit combine with a honeyed finish to create a wonderfully tasty Icewine that tantalizes the taste buds and leaves you yearning for more.

Peller Estates 1999 Andrew Peller Signature Series Riesling Icewine

Niagara Peninsula $$$$ (981175)

This wine is like Arnold Schwarzenegger—big, rich and simple. Huge notes of caramel, peach and apricot open the wine. On the palate, it's finely balanced with a lush, deep flavour profile that carries through to the finish. Not overly complex, but as one panelist said, "There's something to be said for simplicity in Icewine."

Thirty Bench Wines 1999 Riesling Icewine

Niagara Peninsula $$$$ (412932)

A finely crafted wine showcasing the best in Icewine. Opens with an attractive bouquet of lemon, green apple and apricot. On the palate, the acids are higher than most Icewines, but they do a wonderful job of leveling out the residual sugars. With succulent flavours of tropical fruit and a slight oily texture on the finish, this would be the perfect cap to an evening of fine dining with good friends.

RECOMMENDED

Cave Spring Cellars 1999 Riesling Icewine
Niagara Peninsula $$$$ (447441)

A study in complexity would be the best way to describe this wine. With notes of toffee, caramel, apple and pineapple, it doesn't sing Riesling. On the palate, there are hints of citrus flavours heightened by acidity, but it comes across as a little mellow. The long finish captures the senses and brings you back for another sip. Elegant and stylish with substance to back it up.

Harvest Estate Wines 1999 Riesling Icewine
Niagara Peninsula $$$$ (569236)

A shy little fella that doesn't want to come out and play right away. But, once on the palate, this wine becomes the life of the party. Intense flavours of honeydew melon and ripe peach with an under-current of caramel combine to make a delicious wine. Leaning on the thick side, it has enough balance to stay on track from tip to finish.

Henry of Pelham Family Estate Winery 2000 Riesling Icewine
Niagara Peninsula $$$$ (430561)

A well-made wine with typical citrus notes—think lemon pie. Big flavours of apricot, apple and lemon on the palate make it a deliciously tasty wine. With soft acids, this one leans towards the more brash side of Icewine. It's quick to leave the palate, but that is all the more reason to venture back in for another sip.

Hillebrand Estates 1998 Riesling Icewine
Niagara Peninsula $$$$ (980441)
Aging gracefully would be a suitable way to describe this 1998 offering. Soft notes of lemon and pear carry over to the palate. Supple yet light, this Icewine has plenty of acidity, making it almost racy in texture. Still bright and crisp, it could go a few more rounds in the cellar if you're looking to age your Icewine. Subtle hints of petrol are starting to come out and should add to the complexity of the wine.

Jackson-Triggs Okanagan Estate 2000 Proprietors' Grand Reserve Riesling Icewine Okanagan
Okanagan Valley $$$$ (597120)
A tropical delight. Pineapple, mango and lemon notes. Light but good acidity with a crisp mouthfeel. A slight hot touch on the finish gives the palate a little wake-up call. Built to be paired with desserts with a tart touch.

Jackson-Triggs Okanagan Estate 2000 Proprietors' Reserve Riesling Icewine Okanagan
Okanagan Valley $$$$ (597104)

A paint-by-numbers Riesling Icewine. Typical pineapple, lemon and beeswax characteristics. A little on the light side, with acidity playing well off the sugar until the finish, where the sugar hangs around for a while longer. An enjoyable wine for those looking to cap the evening with something tasty but not overpowering.

Pelee Island Winery 2000 Riesling Icewine
Lake Erie North Shore $$$$
Bright citrus characteristics with a touch of peach blossom. Lighter in style, with enough acidity to balance the wine and carry the tropical fruit to the end. A slightly tart finish gives the wine a touch of complexity that would be best enjoyed with citrus-based desserts or fruit platters.

THIRTY BENCH
ICEWINE
2000
RIESLING
VQA NIAGARA PENINSULA VQA
Grown, Produced and Bottled by Thirty Bench
Vineyard and Winery, Beamsville, Ontario
13.0% alc. / vol.   375 ml
White Wine / Vin Blanc
Product of Canada / Produit du Canada

Thirty Bench Wines 2000 Riesling Icewine
Niagara Peninsula $$$$ (412932)
Sipping a well-made Icewine is like listening to
Jesse Cook play the guitar. The playing looks
effortless, but looks are so deceiving. Thirty
Bench's offering comes across as a simple wine,
but once you get into it, you know you're tasting
something special. Trademark notes of caramel
and toffee, with tropical citrus fruit, carry over to
the palate. The flavours burst across the mouth
as the layers of acidity refuse to let the sugar take
over. With its lingering flavour of dried apple on
the crisp finish, this Icewine will put a smile on
your face.

QUITE GOOD

Château des Charmes Winery 1999
Riesling Icewine Paul Bosc Estate Vineyard
Niagara Peninsula $$$$ (413724)
Interesting aged Riesling qualities with petrol,
lemon and beeswax notes. Mellow on the palate,
it's an evenly balanced wine that holds on to its
flinty, citrus characters to the end. Enough weight
and texture to cap off an evening on the patio.

Pillitteri Estates Winery 2000 Riesling Icewine
Niagara Peninsula $$$
Interesting notes of flint and caramel, it has a
spicy flavour that enhances the flinty characters.
A fine line of acidity helps to lift the wine to the
finish. A unique take on Riesling Icewine.

Quails' Gate Estate Winery 2000
Riesling Icewine
Okanagan Valley $$$$ (539239)
It's all about the fruit. Ripe grapefruit, peach and
green apple are the markings of this wine. Sparks
of acidity push the apple juice flavours to the
front, but leave the back a bit shy. A little time in
the bottle should even out this fruity delight.

Other Icewines

HIGHLY RECOMMENDED

Jackson-Triggs Niagara Estate 2000 Proprietors' Grand Reserve Gewürztraminer Icewine

Niagara Peninsula $$$$ (593954)

This Icewine is all about character. With intense aromas of ginger spice and hints of lychee fruit, you know going in it's a Gewürztraminer. On the palate, it's more ginger with apricot and lychee. Finely balanced, this smooth Icewine will have you wanting more. A delicate wine, both unique and delicious.

Jackson-Triggs Niagara Estate 2000 Proprietors' Grand Reserve Cabernet Franc

Niagara Peninsula $$$$ (593962)

If you're looking for a red Icewine that captures the essence of its character, seek this one out. It's a truly masterful wine, with intense raspberry, strawberry and currant notes. On the palate, the Cab Franc characters are heightened by a finely layered balance between the acidity and sugar. Although it's a bit too sweet at first taste, it becomes more integrated on the finish. It would be worth letting it sit in the cellar a bit to see if it can find its balance, but it's still a wonderful companion to a tart dessert dish.

Mission Hill Family Estate Winery 2000 Reserve Chardonnay

Okanagan Valley $$$$ (590497)

Chardonnay is not a widely produced Icewine in Canada, but with so many consumers drinking Chardonnay, it was only a matter of time before Chardonnay Icewine hit the shelves. Mission Hill's offering is indeed a delicious affair with ripe banana, honey and almond notes. Big acidity levels the sugars and gives the wine a crisp edge. Intense plump flavours of banana and lemon wash over the palate with a quick finish. An interesting Icewine best enjoyed in its youth.

RECOMMENDED

Domaine Combret 2000 Saint Vincent Private Reserve Chardonnay Icewine

Okanagan Valley $$$$ (624387)

A solid offering that captures the essence of Chardonnay within the body of an Icewine. Intense notes of butterscotch, pear and pineapple give way to a lighter style of Icewine. A good viscosity on the palate gives the flavours of nutmeg, butterscotch and pear some added depth. With its balanced acidity and sugars, this is a perfect wine for those who enjoy Chardonnay without the woody oak edge. A dash of spice rounds out a well-made wine.

Sumac Ridge Estate Winery 2000 Pinot Blanc Icewine

Okanagan Valley $$$$ (453926)

With a cold snap in early December 2000, the Valley managed to harvest a wide range of grapes from Pinot Noir to Pinot Blanc—and everything in between. The 2000 Pinot Blanc from Sumac Ridge is a tasty wine that comes across as pure baked apple. Although it has a cloying first impression, a crisp mid palate and finish restores the apple flavours. A touch hot on the finish, it's a light enough offering for you to kick back and relax with after a night of entertaining.

QUITE GOOD

Birchwood Estates Wines 2000 Cabernet Franc Icewine

Niagara Peninsula $$$$ (580134)

Soft raspberry and strawberry notes. A little unbalanced, with the acidity splashing across the front of the palate, leaving the sugar to finish the job. Bright fruit up front also tends to fade towards the back, but it's a treat if you're a red wine lover.

Hawthorne Mountain Vineyards 2000 Ehrenfelser Icewine

Okanagan Valley $$$$ (508192)

Produced from a German grape that has found a small home in the Valley, Hawthorne's Ehrenfesler is a fruity mix of papaya, pear and melon. Full of flavour, it has a high sugar-to-acid ratio, giving it a highly sweet taste. If you've got a sweet tooth, this Icewine should fill your sugar craving.

Hernder Estate Winery 1999 Pinot Gris Icewine

Niagara Peninsula $$$$ (563312)

Not a common Icewine in Niagara, Hernder's 1999 is an interesting offering. It's best described as a melting pot of flavours and aromas. From spicy ginger to floral honeysuckle to tropical fruits such as lemon, tangerine and lime, it's a wine that has a bit of everything. A little thin on the palate, which keeps the flavours subdued. A good sipper when chilled down.

Pelee Island Winery 2000 Cabernet Franc Icewine

Lake Erie North Shore $$$$

Overripe strawberry with an earthy character. A tad high on the acid side, it's a hot number that could mellow out with some more time in the bottle. Your best bet is to chill it down and serve with a fresh berry dessert.

Stoney Ridge Cellars 1997 Barrel Fermented Gewürztraminer Icewine

Niagara Peninsula $59.95

If you're looking to see how Icewine can age, check out this 1997 vintage. Having spent time in the barrel, its toasty nut characters have moved to the front of the wine. With hints of raisin aromas, it would be hard to identify this as a G-wine Icewine. The acids are on the decline, but the nutty flavours are still intense. Drinking well now—no need to hold onto this one much longer.

LATE HARVEST WINES

When it comes to Canadian dessert wines, Icewine generally hogs all the attention. Why not? It's got a dramatic storyline. Left behind in the vineyard to face an uncertain future, confined to a mesh prison, defenseless against the peril of ravenous birds and the wintry blasts of inclement weather, the frozen grapes are rescued and pressed under the dark of night to produce one of the world's finest wines.

However, that epic tale comes at a price. The late harvest wines produced in Ontario and British Columbia have no such pedigree. But does that mean we should deny them the love and attention they so richly deserve? We think not.

As Canadian vintners continue to experiment with and improve their production of Icewine, that level of knowledge asserts itself with the wineries' late harvest wines, which can range in sugar levels from

FOOD PAIRING SUGGESTIONS
Remember these wines can be served instead of dessert, as an aperitif or in between courses during a formal dinner. We suggest pairing them with creamy cheeses and a dish of nuts or with fresh fruit desserts that are less sweet than the wine. Salty meats, especially ham or prosciutto, or foie gras would also be a good match for these sweet wines.

medium-sweet sippers to I-can't-believe-it's-not-Icewine sweeties (in the case of Special Select Late Harvest wines).

In general, the results of our panel tasting were quite eye opening—as were the prices. Wineries are turning late harvest Riesling and Vidal into sumptuous wines that are perfectly suited to adding some elegance to your next dinner party. Their lighter-bodied style results in a more food-friendly beverage. They can make a big impression without taxing your budget as much as Icewines, which is something to consider if you took a beating backing Enron or WorldCom.

Riesling and Vidal aren't the only grape varieties allowed to stay out late in the vineyards. There were also a few late harvest Gewürztraminer, Chardonnay, Ehrenfelser, Optima and Ortega vintages that ranked high on our scorecards.

Tasting Panel: LB, RP, WS, CW

VINES AWARD

Cave Spring Cellars 2000 Riesling Indian Summer Select Late Harvest

Niagara Peninsula $$ (415901)

Cave Spring knows Riesling, a fact that is patently clear once you taste this beautifully balanced sweetie. An extremely social late harvest wine, it'll blend in with the food and fun at your dinner table, adding another layer of sophistication to your perfect night at home. Medium-bodied with a plush mouth-feel, it is enhanced by sweet citrus flavours and a lively acidity. It offers strong varietal character—smelling of and tasting like Riesling, especially its aromas of citrus with a hint of petrol and chamomile—and it finishes with a long, lingering nuttiness.

CAVE SPRING

Indian Summer

2000

RIESLING
VQA NIAGARA PENINSULA VQA
Select Late Harvest

CAVE SPRING CELLARS, JORDAN, ONTARIO, CANADA
WHITE WINE/PRODUCT OF CANADA • VIN BLANC/PRODUIT DU CANADA
13.0% alc./vol.   375 mL

St. Hubertus Estate Winery 2001 Summer Symphony

Okanagan Valley $$ (436782)

Although it's labelled a "summer" wine, this late harvest blend is spectacular. Grapes were picked in late January 2002, which means they were destined for Icewine, but unusually warm weather in the Valley forced many wineries to adjust. St. Hubertus simply took in a few different white varietals and presto, a great late harvest wine. It has an attractive fragrance of kiwi, melon and lemon. On the palate, it's a fruit explosion with a great layer of acidity to prop up all the fruit. Lightly sweet, it's the perfect late harvest and a blend to boot. Great for the summer pool party or winter house bash.

HIGHLY RECOMMENDED

Henry of Pelham Family Estate Winery 1999 Riesling Botrytis Affected

Niagara Peninsula $$$ (534628)

A structured and full-bodied late harvest, this deep, delicious wine benefits from the concentrating impact of botrytis (the so-called noble rot which shrivels grapes, compacting their sugars, acidity and flavours). The raisinated grapes produce a honey-like wine, rich and sweet yet beautifully balanced. Pair with desserts using honey and fruit or enjoy chilled by the glass instead of dessert.

Quails' Gate Estate Winery 2001 Late Harvest Optima (Botrytis Affected)

Okanagan Valley $$$ (390328)

The Optima grape is a German hybrid prone to botrytis. This 2001 offering is simply succulent. A bouquet of lily, lilac and honeysuckle resembles the nose of a Muscat. On the palate, it's full of peach, mango and a touch of honey. Light by design since Optima is not a heavy grape, this is a great sipper with a subtle sweet side to it. Opt for this wine if you're in the mood for something decadent yet affordable.

Reif Estate Winery 2000 Special Select Late Harvest Vidal

Ontario $$ (282855)

One of the first wineries in Canada to produce a late harvest Vidal, Reif has been a consistent producer of benchmark classics. The 2000 offering is another gem. Crisp, with bright flavours of apricot, peach and a touch of ginger spice. Amped acidity helps to keep the sugar in check. A delightful treat to sip on its own or enjoy with butterscotch ice cream.

Thirteenth Street Wine Co. 1999 Sandstone Riesling Special Select Late Harvest

Niagara Peninsula $$

Wine can offer many things—from social lubrication to ruminative pleasure. This is a wine with which to ponder the big questions. What happens if an unstoppable force collides with an immovable object? If a tree falls in the forest? Who invented liquid soap? Why? This wonderfully rich and complex late harvest offering lays down waves of interesting and intense flavours on the palate. Very fine, with well-woven sweetness and acidity, it will develop over the short term. Excellent balance, length and value for the price.

Thirty Bench Wines 2000 Riesling Special Select Late Harvest Estate Bottled

Niagara Peninsula $$

One taster dreamed of dispensing this syrupy nectar onto their tongue with an eyedropper, such is its concentrated richness. It's the kind of sugar rush that is extremely tasty, but best enjoyed in small doses. This unbelievably intense, sweet white wine is best partnered with some creamy, runny, stinky cheese— the stinkier the better. An affordable indulgence that's worth the splurge.

Thirty Bench Wines 1999 Riesling Special Select Late Harvest Estate Bottled

Niagara Peninsula $$

Only a lab technician could tell this apart from a Riesling Icewine—it's a fabulous, full, sweet wine with an oily, thick mouth-feel and lovely honeyed citrus and peach flavours. A textbook example of an excellent late harvest wine, it's rich and concentrated but finely balanced with a lively acidity that keeps the sweetness in check. Drink over the next three to five years, perhaps longer. More than a dessert wine, this is dessert.

Vineland Estates Winery 1998 Late Harvest Vidal

Ontario $$

Attractive notes of lemon, grapefruit and peach create an intriguing introduction to a late harvest Vidal. Bright and crisp on the palate, it's a lightweight wine with a fine jab of acidity and sugar. Refined and elegant, this is one Vidal worthy of white linen dinners.

RECOMMENDED

Daniel Lenko Estate Winery 2000 Late Harvest Vidal

Ontario $$

Fresh notes of pineapple, peach and mango. The ripe fruit carries over to the palate with a nice level of acidity. A tad sweet on the front, the acidity takes control through the rest of the wine. Tasty fruit flavours make for a simple sipper that can be brought to the beach or enjoyed while watching *The Sopranos*.

Hawthorne Mountain Vineyards 1998 Late Harvest Optima

Okanagan Valley $$ (536284)

Produced from the Optima grape, which seems to have found a niche following in the Valley, this late harvest offering is full of fruity goodness. Mango and passion fruit dominate from start to finish. With a nice line of acidity and a deft hand with the residual sugar, it's a crisp, fruity wine that would be right at home with Grandma's shortbread cookies. A wine fit for a table cleared of the evening's dinner.

Henry of Pelham Family Estate Winery 2000 Riesling Special Select Late Harvest

Ontario $$ (430579)

Typical late harvest notes of apricot and honey linger behind a strong citrus character in this fresh, smooth-textured wine. The flavours are a bit waxy (not a bad thing) and focussed by a quicksilver thread of acidity, which refreshes the fruit flavours on the finish. Nicely balanced. This wine has potential to develop over the next five years or more.

Henry of Pelham Family Estate Winery 2000 Special Select Late Harvest Vidal

Ontario $$ (395228)

A pineapple delight. Harvested after a couple of frosts, this late harvest was able to gain a few more brix during the extra hang time. Intense like tropical flavoured Jolly Ranchers, there's a lot of acidity in this wine. The extra brix helps to control the acidity, but it's a saucy wine that could use a platter of soft cheese to round out the experience.

Inniskillin Wines 1999 Riesling Special Select Late Harvest

Niagara Peninsula $$$ (560599)

Easily mistaken for a honeyed Icewine, this lush sweetie is a knockout. Subtle aromas of lime and citrus give way to bolder and brighter flavours on the palate. Medium-bodied with a flavourful citrus-tinged finish, this would be an elegant way to start a formal meal. Its intense sweetness would match well with salty foods, such as Roquefort or prosciutto and melon.

Kacaba Vineyards 1999 Late Harvest Vidal

Ontario $$

It's like opening a can of Del Monte fruit cups—rich, lush and full of sweet fruit. Peach, mango and pineapple wash over the palate as ripples of acidity carry the fruit to its spicy finish. A nutty character adds to the overall appeal of the wine. Match with soft cheeses or fruit-based desserts.

Konzelmann Estate Winery 2000 Select Late Harvest Vidal

Ontario $$ (409474)

A deft hand was used to make this late harvest Vidal. Supple fruit flavours of apricot and peach mix with hints of caramel to produce a wonderfully crisp, bright Vidal. With nice layers of acidity to give the wine some depth, this is a fine wine to be enjoyed with good friends and family.

Quails' Gate Estate Winery 2001 Select Late Harvest Riesling

Okanagan Valley $$

Another late harvest that leans towards a well-made Spätlese from Germany. Gorgeous notes of kiwi, lemon and lime peel. On the palate, it's a citrus delight with a rich core of acidity that simply elevates the wine. A dose of residual sugar gives it an added dimension, but doesn't interfere with the overall structure. A delightful wine that would be great to sip as you sit in your favourite chair and catch up on your reading.

Reif Estate Winery 2000 Late Harvest Riesling
Niagara Peninsula $ (282871)

Made in the German "Spätlese" style, which indicates the wine is made from late harvest grapes, but can range from dry to sweet in style. Reif's offering is a lighter-styled wine that is accented by lemon and peach flavours. A nice core of acidity with a touch of residual sugar makes for a pleasurable cocktail wine that would appeal to a wide range of palates. Great match with a mixed cheese platter.

Thomas and Vaughan Vintners 2000 Late Harvest Vidal
Ontario $$

Soft notes of caramel, pineapple and peach. Light and crisp with a racy streak that runs through the core of the wine. Intense fruit flavours coat the palate with a thin layer of residual sugar. A balanced late harvest that could be served as a mid dinner break between entrees.

QUITE GOOD

Black Hills Estate Winery 2001 Sequentia
Okanagan Valley $$$

A 100 per cent Sauvignon Blanc late harvest. Although it has a funky nose of cut grass that's been in the sun for a while, on the palate, it's more intense and flavourful. The typical grassy flavours with lemon peel are common to the Sauvignon Blanc grape. A little out of whack with the acidity, it has an interesting herbaceous finish to it. One to try if you're at the winery.

Blossom Winery 2000 Riesling Select Late Harvest
British Columbia $$$ (627570)

A lean, off-dry Riesling with positive apple flavours and a warm finish. Only moderately sweet, this is an extremely versatile wine that would work well with a wide variety of dishes, including mild curries and ginger-flavoured dishes.

Château des Charmes Winery 1998 Riesling Late Harvest Estate Bottled
Niagara Peninsula $$ (432930)

Honey and toffee-like aromas intermingle with some toast and citrus notes in this sweet wine. On the palate, flavours of lemon blossom and dried apricot emerge. The texture is full and rich, balanced by a zesty acidity.

Colio Estate Vineyards 2000 Late Harvest Vidal
Ontario $ (470369)

A little on the light side, this wine has some core fruit of peach and ripe apricot, but it lacks intensity. Streaks of acidity help to lift the fruit, but it falls a bit short of a finish. A punch of spice adds some interest. Try matching with spicy Thai dishes—it may just work.

Strewn Wines 1998 Late Harvest Vidal
Ontario $$ (527755)

Flashes of caramel, peach and apricot come out of this wine. It's a lean offering that has concentrated flavours, but not enough acidity to boost the wine up. A quick sipper for watching with *The National*.

REFERENCE SOURCES FOR CANADIAN WINES

PRINTED RESOURCES

Vintage Canada:
The Complete Guide to Canadian
Wines, 3rd edition
by Tony Aspler
McGraw-Hill Ryerson, 1999

Chardonnay and Friends:
Varietal Wines of British Columbia
by John Schreiner
Orca Book Publishers, 1999

Icewine: The Complete Story
by John Schreiner
Warwick Pulications, 2001

Canadian Wine for Dummies
by Tony Aspler and Barbara Leslie
CDG Books Canada, 2000

Touring Niagara's Wine Country
by Linda Bramble
James Lorimer & Co., 2000

Oxford Companion to the Wines
of North America
edited by Bruce Cass, with
consultant editor, Jancis Robinson
Oxford University Press, 2000

PUBLICATIONS

Vines magazine
159 York Street, St. Catharines,
 ON L2R 6E9
Toll-free 1-888-883-3372
Telephone 905-682-4509
www.vinesmag.com
For a free copy of *Vines*, contact us.

BC Wine Trails
P.O. Box 1319, Summerland, BC
 V08 1Z0
Telephone: 250-494-7733
Fax: 250-494-7737
www.bcwine.com/trails

WEB SITES

www.canwine.com
www.vancouver-island-bc.com/
 canadianwines/viwines.htm
www.wineroute.com
www.winesofcanada.com
www.bcwine.com
www.brocku.ca/ccovi
www.agsci.ubc.ca/wine

GLOSSARY

Acid/Acidic: Tart, sour or even fresh character, which has an impact on the body, balance and longevity of wine. Generally more obvious in and more descriptive of young white wines, where it gives balance and a crisp, clean taste.

Alcohol: What separates wine from grape juice, alcohol is expressed in per cent by volume of the total liquid and is a key flavour component and preservative. Canadian table wines generally range from ten to fourteen per cent.

Aroma: The range of scents found in a wine, including primary fruit aromas from the grape, secondary aromas from winemaking, and tertiary aromas from bottle aging.

Balance/Balanced: Positive assessment of a wine's character, essentially all of its components (fruit, acid/tannin, and finish) are in harmony.

Barnyard/Farmyard/Stables: Description of a decidedly complex and funky animal aroma found in some red wines. In lay terms could be assessed as smelling of poo, but tasting of heaven. Fear not, these descriptors always sound more off-putting than they actually are.

Barrel/Barriques: Wooden barrels, commonly produced by makers in France, America and, to a smaller degree Hungary and Yugoslavia, are made from oak staves and toasted on the inside for the aging of wine. With a lifespan of four or five years, barrels are expensive (generally $650 to $1,000 per 225 litre (60 gallon) barrel) so are generally used only for wines with the inherent quality for long-term cellaring, a major reason "Barrel Aged," "Barrel Fermented" and "Barrel Reserve" wines cost you more. The newer the barrel the more oak flavouring imparted in the wine.

Barrel Aged: Any wine that was aged in a barrel after the completion of fermentation, anywhere from a few months to several years. Generally, barrel aged wines have more noticeable oak character than barrel fermented wines.

Barrel Fermented: Any wine, though usually exclusive white wine (Chardonnay, Sauvignon Blanc or, in one rare case, Riesling), fermented in oak barrels as opposed to stainless steel or other fermentation tanks. Perhaps surprisingly, although this process adds to the body and mouth-feel, it doesn't necessarily impart oak characteristics to the finished wine.

Blend: A wine that is blended from different grapes, vineyards, wine regions or vintages. It's a case of the sum being better than its parts, different wines mixed together to create the best wine possible. The practice is most transparent in varietal wine such as Cabernet/Merlot or Riesling/Gewürztraminer, however most every wine is a blend.

Body: How the wine feels on the palate, which ranges from light to heavy (or full-bodied).

Botrytis Affected (BA)/Botrytis Cinerea: A beneficial rot that shrivels the grapes and concentrates their flavour, sugar and acidity. Botrytis plays a role in some late harvest wines and Icewines produced in Ontario and British Columbia.

Brix: Term for natural grape sugar, often an indicator of ripeness of the fruit since warmer growing seasons produce higher sugar levels.

Brut: French for dry, used to identify dry sparkling wine.

Buttery: Rich, creamy aroma, flavour and texture associated with malolactic fermentation, a winemaking process that converts hard, malic acid (green apple flavours) in wine to soft, lactic acid (rich, butter flavours).

Cedar: Aroma in wine imparted by oak aging.

Character: Distinct attributes of a wine or grape variety.

Closed: Not revealing aromas or flavours. Aging and/or decanting can help it "open up."

Complex: Praiseworthy wine that displays layered aromas, flavours and texture.

Creamy: Description of a wine's mouth-feel, which is akin to cream; doesn't imply lactic flavour.

Cuvé Close: Affordable and fast sparkling wine fermentation technique in which the secondary fermentation is done in a reinforced stainless steel tank; also known as the Charmat process.

Cuvée: Blend of wines from the same region.

Decanting: Simply pouring wine from the bottle to another container in order to aerate the wine and remove sediment, usually reserved exclusively for red wines other than Gamay and Pinot Noir.

Dry: No sugar or residual sweetness remaining (note that a fruity wine can be dry).

Dusty: Refers to the drying effect of tannin in red wine.

Earthy: Describes complex and appealing aromas and flavours such as mushroom, mineral or earth.

Estate Bottled: Labelling prerogative for wineries that grow, vinify and bottle grapes from their own vineyards, generally a sign of quality wine.

Finish: The final flavour impression a wine makes, ranging from short to long duration.

Firm: Describes the texture and structure of a wine, usually young tannic reds that show great potential for the future.

Gamy: Meaty, slightly decaying aromas resembling game meats found in complex reds, another strangely appealing quality given the right dosage.

Grassy: Aromas and flavours of fresh-cut grass or fresh herbs, most descriptive of Sauvignon Blanc.

Green: Unripe, tart flavours and textures usually caused by unripe grapes.

Grip/Gripping: The firmness of tannin (red wine) or acidity (white) on the palate, considered a good indication of a well-made wine.

Herbaceous: A vegetal, grassy, herbal tone in aromas and flavours.

Icewine: Protected term that describes late harvest wines produced from naturally frozen grapes on the vine.

Jammy: Rich, concentrated, semi-sweet fruit character.

Late Harvest: Term with far-reaching application and source of much confusion on wine labels, essentially meaning grapes were left on the vine after normal harvest time. Most late harvest wines enjoy dramatically increased sweetness and flavours, but not all.

Lean: Describes a wine with more acidity than fruit, not necessarily a flaw.

Length/Lingering/Long: Measurement of a wine's final impression after swallowing, following the logic that the longer the finish, the better the wine.

Mellow: Soft, well-balanced wine that lacks intensity, not necessarily a flaw.

Meritage: American term, which rhymes with "heritage" and describes red or white blended wines made in the fashion of Bordeaux, generally a premium wine produced in small batches in better vintages.

Malolactic Fermentation: A secondary fermentation, used to soften some Chardonnay and red wines, whereby the malic acid of the wine is converted to lactic acid.

Mouth-feel: Describes the texture of the wine on the palate.

Non-vintage: A wine produced by blending wines from different years, such as sparkling wines designed in a house style that is unchanging from bottle to bottle, year to year.

Nose: The smells and aromas of a wine.

Old Vines: Wine produced from vineyards planted longer than fifteen years ago, the older a vine gets the less fruit it produces, the less fruit on a vine, the more concentrated the flavours, sugars and acidity.

Palate: Overarching term referring to both the wine's flavour and the mechanics of tasting.

Petrol/Kerosene: Pungent yet pleasant gasoline and oil aromas most typical of maturing or mature Riesling.

Racy: Describes lively, zesty acidity, most often found in Riesling and Sauvignon Blanc.

Reserve: Unregulated term that suggests the wine has received much tender loving care from the winemaker—ideally, it highlights a winery's best bottles.

Round: Smooth flavours and texture in a well-balanced wine.

Single Vineyard: Means 100 per cent of the grapes came from the same vineyard, usually an indicator of premium quality.

Smoky: Describes aromas of smoke generally imparted in the wine via oak aging.

Sur Lie or Sur Lee: French term describing winemaking technique of aging wine on the lees (spent yeast cells) to contribute nutty, yeasty character.

Süssreserve: The winemaker reintroduced some unfermented grape juice into the wine before bottling. It adds some sweetness and can enhance the roundness of the mouth-feel.

Tannin: Drying, astringent texture derived from grapes and barrels, which adds structure to full-bodied red wine.

Tart: Puckering acidity, considered a fault if excessive.

Terroir: A controversial French term suggesting that certain vineyards impart a unique character to the wines they produce which cannot be duplicated anywhere else, with the quality of the soil and the wind, rain and other climatic conditions adding their signature to the finished wine. New World critics dismiss it as a marketing ploy, but a growing number of winemakers are subscribing to the theory, as they identify vineyards that year-in, year-out, produce better fruit and in turn better wine than other sites.

Texture: Overall mouth-feel of the wine, including all components (tannin, acidity, fruit extract and concentration).

Toasty: Pleasant aroma in wine imparted by oak barrels.

Varietal: Wine named after its principal grape, such as Chardonnay or Cabernet Franc. According to the VQA it must contain at least eighty per cent of that grape blended with twenty per cent other accepted varieties.

Vintage: Year in which grapes were harvested; in the case of Icewine production, which often carries over into a new year, the vintage date doesn't roll over.

VQA: Vintners Quality Alliance—winemaking standards, produced and legislated in Ontario and adopted in British Columbia, that cover designated growing regions, grape varieties and accepted practices,

Warm: Describes a wine with noticeable heat from its alcohol content, considered a fault if the perception passes warm to become hot.

Yeasty: Fresh dough/biscuit-like aromas and flavours, more acceptable when found in sparkling wine.

Zesty/Zippy: Describes lively, fresh acidity.

CANADIAN WINERIES

British Columbia

VANCOUVER ISLAND

Alderlea Vineyards
1751 Stamps Rd., RR1, Duncan
T: 250.746.7122
F: 250.746.7122

Blue Grouse Vineyards and Winery
4365 Blue Grouse Rd., Duncan
T: 250.743.3834
F: 250.743.9305
E: skiltz@islandnet.com
www.bluegrousevineyards.com

Chalet Estate Vineyard
11195 Chalet Rd., North Saanich
T: 250.656.2552
F: 250.656.9719
E: chaletestate@shaw.ca
www.chaletestatevineyard.ca

Chateau Wolff
2534 Maxey Rd., Nanaimo
T: 250.753.9669
F: 250.753.0614

Cherry Point Vineyards
840 Cherry Point Rd., RR3,
  Cobble Hill
T: 250.743.1272
F: 250.743.1059
E: ulrich@islandnet.com
www.cherrypointvineyards.com

Glenterra Vineyards
3897 Cobble Hill Rd., Cobble Hill
T: 250.743.2330
F: 250.743.2496
E: glenterravineyards@shaw.ca

Saturna Island Vineyards
8 Quarry Trail, Saturna Island
T: 1.877.918.3388
F: 250.539.3515
E: wine@saturnavineyards.com
www.saturnavineyards.com

Venturi-Schulze Vineyards
4235 Trans Canada Hwy., RR1,
  Cobble Hill
T: 250.743.5630
F: 250.743.5638
E: info@venturischulze.com
www.veturischulze.com

FRASER VALLEY

Andrés Wines
2120 Vitner St., Port Moody
T: 604.937.3411
F: 604.937.5487
E: info@andreswines.com

Blossom Winery
5491 Minoru Blvd., Richmond
T: 604.232.9839
E: blossomwinery@telus.net
www.blossomwinery.com

Domaine de Chaberton Estates
1064 216th St., Langley
T: 1.888.332.9463
F: 604.533.9687
E: info@domainedechaberton.com
www.domainedechaberton.com

Township 7 Vineyards and Winery
21152 16th Ave., Langley
T: 604.532.1766
F: 604.532.1752
E: wine@township7.com
www.township7.com

OKANAGAN VALLEY

Benchland Vineyards
170 Upper Bench Rd. South, Penticton
T: 250.770.1733
F: 250.770.1734

Black Hill Estate Winery
30880 Black Sage Rd., RR1
S52, C22, Oliver
T: 250.498.0666
F: 250.498.0690
E: info@blackhillswinery.com
www.blackhillswinery.com

Blasted Church Winery
378 Parson Rd., Okanagan Falls
T: 250.497.1125
F: 250.497.1126

Blue Mountain Vineyard
RR1, S3, C4, Okanagan Falls
T: 250.497.8244
F: 250.497.6160
E: bluemountain@
bluemountainwinery.com
www.bluemountainwinery.com

Burrowing Owl Estate Winery
100 Burrowing Owl Place, RR1
S52, C20, Oliver
T: 877.498.0620
F: 250.498.0621
E: info@bovwine.com

Calona Vineyards
1125 Richter St., Kelowna
T: 888.246.4472
F: 250.762.2999
E: wineboutique@cascadia.ca

Carriage House Wines
Black Sage Rd., RR1, S46, C19, Oliver
T: 250.498.8818
F: 250.498.8818
E: carhsewines@otvcablelan.net

CedarCreek Estate Winery
5445 Lakeshore Rd., Kelowna
T: 250.764.8866
F: 250.764.2603
E: info@cedarcreek.bc.ca
www.cedarcreek.bc.ca

Domaine Combret
Box 1170
131st St. North/Rd. 13, Oliver
T: 250.498.8878
F: 250.498.8879
E: info@combretwine.com
www.combretwine.com

Fairview Cellars
RR1, S66, C15, Oliver
T: 250.498.2211
F: 250.498.2130
E: beggert@img.net

Gehringer Brothers Estate Winery
Rd. 8, RR1, S23, C4, Oliver
T: 250.498.3537
F: 2350.498.3510

Gray Monk Estate Winery
1055 Camp Rd., Okanagan Centre
T: 1.800.663.4205
F: 250.766.3390
E: mailbox@graymonk.com
www.graymonk.com

Hawthorne Mountain Vineyards
Green Lake Rd., Box 480,
    Okanagan Falls
T: 250.497.8267
F: 250.497.8073
E: hawthorn@vip.net
www.hmvineyard.com

Hester Creek Estate Winery
13163 326th St., Oliver
T: 250.498.4435
F: 250.498.0651
E: info@hestercreek.com
www.hestercreek.com

Hillside Estate Winery
1350 Naramata Rd., Penticton
T: 1.888.923.9463
F: 250.493.6294
E: klauzon@hillsideestate.com
www.hillsideestate.com

House of Rose Winery
2270 Garner Rd., Kelowna
T: 250.765.0802
F: 250.765.7762
E: arose@shuswap.net

Inniskillin Okanagan Vineyards
Road 11 West, RR1 S24, C5, Oliver
T: 1.800.498.6211
F: 250.498.4566
www.inniskillin.com

Jackson-Triggs Okanagan
Highway 97, PO Box 1650, Oliver
T: 250.498.4981
F: 250.498.6505
www.atlaswine.com

Kettle Valley Winery
RR1, S2, C39, Naramata
T: 250.496.5898
F: 250.496.5298
E: kettlevalleywinery@telus.net

Lang Vineyards Ltd.
2493 Gammon Rd., RR1, S11, C55,
  Naramata
T: 250.496.5987
F: 250.496.5706
www.langvineyards.com

Mission Hill Family Estate
1730 Mission Hill, Westbank
T: 250.768.7611
F: 250.768.2267
E: info@missionhillwinery.com
www.missionhillwinery.com

Mt. Boucherie Estate Winery
829 Douglas Rd., Kelowna
T: 250.769.8803
F: 250.769.9330
E: sales@mtboucherie.bc.ca
www.mtboucherie.bc.ca

Nichol Vineyard
RR1, S14, C13, 1285 Smethurst
  Rd., Naramata
T: 250.496.5962
F: 250.496.4275

Paradise Ranch Vineyards
Naramata Rd., Naramata
T: 604.683.6040
F: 604.683.8611
E: info@icewines.com
www.icewines.com

Pentâge Wines
4400 Lakeside Rd., Penticton
T: 250.493.4008
F: 250.493.4008
E: pentage@vip.net
www.pentagewines.com

Pinot Reach Cellars
1670 Dehart Rd., Kelowna
T: 250.764.0078
F: 250.764.0771
E: pinot@direct.ca
www.pinotreach.com

Quails' Gate Estate Winery
3303 Boucherie Rd., Kelowna
T: 250.769.4451
F: 250.769.3451
E: info@quailsgate.com
www.quailsgate.com

Recline Ridge Winery
RR1, S12, C16, Tappen
T: 250.835.2212
F: 250.835.2228
E: inquiry@recline-ridge.bc.ca
www.recline-ridge.bc.ca

Red Rooster Winery
910 Debeck Rd., Naramata
T: 250.496.4041
F: 250.496.5674
E: redrooster@img.net
www.redroosterwinery.com

St. Hubertus Estate Winery
5225 Lakeshore Rd., Kelowna
T: 1.800.989.9463
F: 250.764.0499
E: wine@st-hubertus.bc.ca
www.st-hubertus.bc.ca

Silver Sage Winery
32032 87th St., Oliver
T: 250.498.0310
E: silversagewinery@hotmail.com

Sumac Ridge Estate Winery
Highway 97, PO Box 307,
 Summerland
T: 250.494.0451
F: 250.494.3456
E: sumac@vip.net
www.sumacridge.com

Thornhaven Estates Winery
6816 Andrew Ave., Summerland
T: 250.494.7778
F: 250.494.8683
E: sales@thornhaven.com
www.thornhaven.com

Tinhorn Creek Vineyards
32830 Tinhorn Creek Rd.,
 PO Box 2010, Oliver
T: 1.888.484.6467
F: 250.498.3228
E: winery@tinhorn.com
www.tinhorn.com

Wild Goose Vineyards
2145 Sun Valley Way, RR1, S3,
 C11, Okanagan Falls
T: 250.497.8919
F: 250.497.6853
E: info@wildgoosewinery.com
www.wildgoosewinery.com

ONTARIO

NIAGARA PENINSULA

Andrés Wines
697 South Service Rd., Grimsby
T: 1.800.836.3555
F: 905.643.4944

Angels Gate Winery
4260 Mountainview Rd.,
 Beamsville
T: 905.563.3942
F: 905.563.4127

Birchwood Estate Winery
4676 Cherry Ave., Vineland
T: 905.562.8463
F: 905.562.6344
E: agreen@diamondwines.com
www.birchwoodwines.com

Cave Spring Cellars
3836 Main St., Jordan
T: 905.562.3581
F: 905.562.3232
E: cscwine@cavespringcellars.com
www.cavespringcellars.com

Château des Charmes Winery
1025 York Rd., Niagara-on-the-Lake
T: 905.262.4219
F: 905.262.5548
E: info@chateaudescharmes.com
www.chateaudescharmes.com

Creekside Estate Winery
2170 4th Ave., Jordan Station
T: 1.877.262.9463
F: 905.562.5493
www.creeksideestatewinery.com

Crown Bench Estates Winery
3850 Aberdeen Rd., Beamsville
T: 905.563.3959
F: 905.563.3441
E: winery@crownbenchestates.com
www.crownbenchestates.com

Daniel Lenko Estate Winery
5246 Regional Rd. 81, Beamsville
T: 905.563.7756
www.daniellenko.com

EastDell Estates
4041 Locust Lane, Beamsville
T: 905.563.9463
F: 905.563.1241
E: winery@eastdell.com
www.eastdell.com

Featherstone Estate Winery
3678 Victoria Ave., Vineland
T: 905.562.1949
F: 905.562.3989

Harbour Estates Winery
4362 Jordan Rd., Jordan Station
T: 1.877.439.9463
F: 905.562.3829
E: info@hewwine.com
www.hewwine.com

Harvest Estate Wines
1179 4th Ave., St. Catharines
T: 905.684.3300
E: wine@vaxxine.com

Henry of Pelham Family Estate Winery
1469 Pelham Rd., St. Catharines
T: 905.684.8423
F: 905.684.8444
E: winery@henryofpelham.com
www.henryofpelham.com

Hernder Estate Winery
1607 8th Ave., St. Catharines
T: 905.684.3300
F: 905.684.3303
E: wine@vaxxine.com
www.hernder.com

Hillebrand Estates
1249 Niagara Stone Rd.,
  Highway 55, RR2,
  Niagara-on-the-Lake
T: 1.800.582.8412
E: info@hillebrand.com
www.hillebrand.com

Inniskillin Wines
Niagara Parkway at Line 3, RR1,
  Niagara-on-the-Lake
T: 905.468.3554
F: 905.468.5355
E: inniskil@inniskillin.com
www.inniskillin.com

Jackson-Triggs Niagara Estates
2145 Niagara Stone Rd., Highway
  55, Niagara-on-the-Lake
T: 905.564.3003
E: info@jacksontriggswinery.com
www.jacksontriggswinery.com

Joseph's Estate Winery
1811 Niagara Stone Rd.,
    Highway 55, RR3,
    Niagara-on-the-Lake
T: 905.468.1259
F: 905.468.9242
E: info@josephsestatewines.com
www.josephsestatewines.com

Kacaba Vineyards
3550 King St., Vineland
T: 905.562.5625
F: 416.361.1776
E: mikelachance@sympatico.com
www.kacabavineyards.com

Konzelmann Estate Winery
1696 Lakeshore Rd.,
    Niagara-on-the-Lake
T: 905.935.2866
F: 905.935.2864
E: wine@konzelmannwines.com
www.konzelmannwines.com

Lakeview Cellars
4037 Cherry Ave., Vineland
T: 905.562.5685
F: 905.562.0673
E: lakecell@lakeviewcellars.on.ca
www.lakeviewcellars.on.ca

Magnotta Cellars
4701 Ontario St., Beamsville
T: 905.563.5313
F: 905.738.5551
E: info@magnotta.com
www.magnotta.com

Maleta Vineyards
450 Queenston Rd., RR4,
    Niagara-on-the-Lake
T: 605.685.8486
F: 905.685.7998

Malivoire Wine Company
4260 King St. E., Regional Rd. 81,
    Beamsville
T: 905.563.9253
F: 905.563.9512
E: ladybug@malivoirewineco.com
www.malivoirewineco.com

Marynissen Estates
RR6, Concession 1,
    Niagara-on-the-Lake
T: 905.468.7270
F: 905.468.5784
www.marynissenestates.com

Peller Estates
290 John St., Niagara-on-the-Lake
T: 1.888.673.5537
E: info@pellar.com
www.peller.com

Peninsula Ridge Estates Winery
5600 King St. W., Regional Rd. 81,
    Beamsville
T: 905.563.0900
F: 905.563.0995
E: info@peninsularidge.com
www.peninsularidge.com

Pillitteri Estate Winery
696 Highway 55, RR2,
Niagara-on-the-Lake
T: 905.468.3147
F: 905.468.0389
E: winery@pillitteri.com
www.pillitteri.com

Puddicombe Estate Winery
1468 Highway 8, Winona
T: 905.643.1015
F: 905.468.5878
E: puddicombe_farms@hotmail.com
www.puddicombefarms.com

Reif Estate Winery
15608 Niagara Parkway, RR1,
Niagara-on-the-Lake
T: 905.468.7738
F: 905.468.5878
E: wine@reifwinery.com
www.reifwinery.com

Rockway Glen Estate Winery
3290 9th St., St. Catharines
T:905.641.5771
F: 905.641.2031
E: rockway@niagara.com
www.rockwayglen.com

Royal DeMaria Wines
4551 Cherry Ave., Vineland
T: 905.562.6767
F: 905.562.6775
E: icewine@royaldemaria.com
www.royaldemaria.com

Stonechurch Vineyards
1270 Irvine Rd., RR5,
Niagara-on-the-Lake
T: 905.935.3535
F: 905.646.8892
E: wine@stonechurch.com
www.stonechurch.com

Stoney Ridge Cellars
3201 King St., Regional Rd. 81,
Vineland
T: 905.562.1324
F: 905.562.7777
E: srcellar@vaxxine.com
www.stoneyridge.com

Strewn Wines
1339 Lakeshore Rd.,
Niagara-on-the-Lake
T: 905.468.1229
F: 905.468.8305
E: info@strewnwinery.com
www.strewnwinery.com

Thirteenth Street Wine Co.
13th St. South, RR1, Jordan
Station
T: 905.562.9463
E: funkwine@vaxxine.com

Thirty Bench Wines
4281 Mountainview Rd.,
Beamsville
T: 905.563.1698
F: 905.563.3921
E: wine@thirtybench.com
www.thirtybench.com

Thomas & Vaughan Vintners
4245 King St., Regional Rd. 81,
    Beamsville
T: 905.563.7737
F: 905.563.4114
E: info@thomasandvaughan.com
www.thomasandvaughan.com

Vineland Estates Winery
3620 Moyer Rd., RR1, Vineland
T: 905-562.7088
F: 905.562.3071
E: wine@vineland.com
www.vineland.com

Willow Heights Winery
3751 Regional Rd. 81, RR1,
    Vineland
T: 905.562.4945
F: 905.562.5761
E: willow.heights@sympatico.ca
www.willowheightswinery.on.ca

LAKE ERIE NORTH SHORE

Colio Estate Vineyards
1 Colio Dr., Harrow
T: 1.800.265.1322
F: 519.738.3070
E: colio@total.net
www.colio.com

Grape Tree Estate Winery
308 Mersea Rd. 3, Leamington
T: 519.322.2081
E: winery@grapetreewines.com
www.grapetreewines.com

Pelee Island Winery
455 Seacliff Dr., Kingsville
T: 1.800.597.3533
E: pelee@peleeisland.com
www.peleeisland.com

TORONTO

Cilento Wines
672 Chrislea Rd., Woodbridge
T: 1.888.245.9463
E: cilento@ica.net
www.cliento.com

Southbrook Winery
1061 Major Mackenzie Dr., Maple
T: 905.832.2548
F: 905.832.9811
E: office@southbrook.com
www.southbrook.com

INDEX OF WINERIES

INDEX OF WINES

Hester Creek Estate Winery 1999 Pinot Blanc 67

Hester Creek Estate Winery 2000 Cabernet-Merlot 157

Hester Creek Estate Winery 2000 Merlot 166

Hester Creek Estate Winery 2000 Pinot Gris 73

Hillebrand Estates 1997 Glenlake Vineyard Merlot Unfiltered 175

Hillebrand Estates 1998 Riesling Icewine 217

Hillebrand Estates 1999 Showcase Merlot Glenlake Vineyard 170

Hillebrand Estates 1999 Trius Vidal Icewine 213

Hillebrand Estates 2000 Harvest Gamay 195

Hillebrand Estates Winery 1995 Showcase Cabernet Franc Unfiltered Glenlake Vineyard 135

Hillebrand Estates Winery 1997 Showcase Cabernet Franc Unfiltered Glenlake Vineyard 139

Hillebrand Estates Winery 1997 Trius Chardonnay Beamsville Bench Barrel Fermented 51

Hillebrand Estates Winery 1997 Trius Red 157

Hillebrand Estates Winery 1999 Showcase Cabernet Franc Unfiltered Glenlake Vineyard 134

Hillebrand Estates Winery 1999 Showcase Cabernet Sauvignon Glenlake Vineyard 145

Hillebrand Estates Winery 1999 Showcase Chardonnay Unfiltered (Wine Bottled with Its Lees) 42

Hillebrand Estates Winery 1999 Trius Grand Red 155

Hillebrand Estates Winery 2000 Chardonnay Collector's Choice Barrel Aged 50

Hillebrand Estates Winery 2000 Pinot Gris Vineyard Select 79

Hillebrand Estates Winery 2000 Showcase Chardonnay Barrel 4089 (New Troncais Oak) Glenlake Vineyard 41

Hillebrand Estates Winery 2000 Showcase Chardonnay Barrel 4094 (New Troncais Oak) 41

Hillebrand Estates Winery 2000 Showcase Chardonnay Barrel 4099 (New Troncais Oak) Huebel Vineyard 50

Hillebrand Estates Winery 2000 Showcase Chardonnay Barrel 9017 (Old American Oak) 37

Hillebrand Estates Winery 2000 Trius Chardonnay Beamsville Bench 42

Hillebrand Estates Winery 2000 Trius Chardonnay Lakeshore 42

Hillebrand Estates Winery 2001 Gamay Noir Rosé Vineyard Select 126

Hillebrand Estates Winery 2001 Muscat Reserve Vineyard Select 109

Hillebrand Estates Winery 2001 Sauvignon Blanc Vineyard Series 99

Hillebrand Estates Winery 2001 Trius Riesling Dry 88

Hillebrand Estates Winery Trius Brut NV 117

Hillside Estate 2000 Merlot Reserve 171

Hillside Estate 2001 Gamay Blush 124

Hillside Estate 2001 Gewürztraminer 64

Hillside Estate 2001 Muscat Ottonel 109

House of Rose Winery 1998 Sémillon—The Green Rose 110

Inniskillin Okanagan Vineyards 1998 Pinot Noir Estate Bottled 183

Inniskillin Wines Okanagan Vineyards 1999 Pinot Noir Estate Bottled 183

Inniskillin Okanagan Vineyards 1999 Reserve Chardonnay 42

Inniskillin Okanagan Vineyards 1999 Reserve Meritage 157

Inniskillin Wines Okanagan Vineyards 2000 Riesling Icewine Dark Horse Estate Vineyard 214

Inniskillin 1999 Cabernet Franc Reserve 132

Inniskillin Vineyards 1999 Cabernet Sauvignon Klose Vineyard 142

Inniskillin Wines 1999 Chardonnay Founders' Reserve Chardonnay 43

Inniskillin Wines 1999 Chardonnay Reserve 43

Inniskillin Wines 1999 Founders' Reserve Pinot Noir 183

Inniskillin Wines 1999 Reserve Meritage 158

Inniskillin Wines 1999 Riesling Special Select Late Harvest 229

Inniskillin Wines 1999 Schuele Vineyard Merlot 175

Inniskillin Wines 2000 Brae Burn Estate Shiraz 199

Inniskillin Wines 2000 Chardonnay Klose Vineyard 42

Inniskillin Wines 2000 Chardonnay Seeger Vineyard 35

Inniskillin Wines 2000 Montague Estate Vineyard Pinot Noir 184

Inniskillin Wines 2000 Pinot Noir 187

Inniskillin Wines 2000 Riesling 88

Inniskillin Wines 2000 Travigne (White) 113

Inniskillin Wines 2000 Vidal Icewine 211

Inniskillin Wines 2001 Pinot Grigio 79

Inniskillin Wines 2001 Riesling Late Autumn 91

Jackson-Triggs Niagara Estate 1999 Proprietors' Grand Reserve Meritage 158

Jackson-Triggs Niagara Estate 2000 Proprietors' Grand Reserve Cabernet Franc Icewine 219

Marynissen Estates 2000 Pinot Noir Butler's Grant Vineyard 184

Marynissen Estates 2000 Riesling Marynissen Vineyard 92

Marynissen Estates 2001 Sauvignon Blanc 99

Mission Hill 49 N 1999 Chardonnay, Pinot Blanc, Semillon 115

Mission Hill Cordillera 2001 Spotted Lake Sauvignon Blanc 97

Mission Hill Cordillera Okanagan 2001 Wild Horse Canyon 113

Mission Hill Family Estate Winery 1998 Reserve Vidal Icewine 212

Mission Hill Family Estate Winery 1999 Cabernet Sauvignon Reserve 143

Mission Hill Family Estate Winery 1999 Merlot 165

Mission Hill Family Estate Winery 1999 Oculus 153

Mission Hill Family Estate Winery 1999 Pinot Gris Reserve 77

Mission Hill Family Estate Winery 1999 Reserve Merlot 172

Mission Hill Family Estate Winery 1999 Shiraz Reserve 199

Mission Hill Family Estate Winery 1999 Syrah Estate 199

Mission Hill Family Estate Winery 2000 Cabernet/Merlot 160

Mission Hill Family Estate Winery 2000 Chardonnay Bin 99 52

Mission Hill Family Estate Winery 2000 Chardonnay Reserve 44

Mission Hill Family Estates Winery 2000 Merlot 176

Mission Hill Family Estate Winery 2000 Pinot Blanc 69

Mission Hill Family Estate Winery 2000 Pinot Gris 74

Mission Hill Family Estate Winery 2000 Pinot Gris Reserve 185

Mission Hill Family Estate Winery 2000 Pinot Noir Bin 99 185

Mission Hill Family Estate Winery 2000 Reserve Chardonnay 220

Mission Hill Family Estate Winery 2000 Reserve Pinot Noir 77

Mission Hill Family Estate Winery 2000 Sauvignon Blanc Reserve 99

Mission Hill Family Estate Winery 2001 Gewürztraminer 58

Mission Hill Family Estate Winery 2001 Pinot Blanc 69

Mission Hill Family Estate Winery 2001 Pinot Grigio 73

Mission Hill Family Estate Winery 2001 Pinot Gris Reserve 77

Mission Hill Family Estate Winery 2001 Riesling Dry 93

Pelee Island Winery 2000 Baco Noir 202

Pelee Island Winery 2000 Cabernet Franc Icewine 221

Pelee Island Winery 2000 Pinot Noir 188

Pelee Island Winery 2000 Riesling Icewine 217

Pelee Island Winery 2000 Vinedressers Merlot 172

Peller Estates 1998 Private Reserve Cabernet Franc 139

Peller Estates 1998 Private Reserve Cabernet Sauvignon 143

Peller Estates 1999 Andrew Peller Signature Series Cabernet Franc Unfiltered 135

Peller Estates 1999 Andrew Peller Signature Series Cabernet Sauvignon 143

Peller Estates 1999 Andrew Peller Signature Series Chardonnay Sur Lie 53

Peller Estates 1999 Andrew Peller Signature Series Merlot 173

Peller Estates 1999 Andrew Peller Signature Series Riesling Icewine 215

Peller Estates 1999 Private Reserve Cabernet Franc 139

Peller Estates 1999 Private Reserve Chardonnay Barrel-Aged 45

Peller Estates 1999 Private Reserve Merlot 173

Peller Estates 2000 Private Reserve Dry Riesling 89

Peller Estates 2000 Private Reserve Pinot Noir 188

Peller Estates 2000 Private Reserve Sauvignon Blanc Barrel Aged 97

Peller Estates 2000 Vineyard Series Gamay Noir 195

Peller Estates 2000 Vineyard Series Muscat 107

Peller Estates Founder's Series Cristalle 117

Peller Estates Okanagan 2000 Private Reserve Barrel-Aged Merlot 176

Peller Estates Okanagan 2000 Private Reserve Pinot Noir 181

Peninsula Ridge Estates Winery 2000 Cabernet 158

Peninsula Ridge Estates Winery 2000 Cabernet Franc Reserve 131

Peninsula Ridge Estates Winery 2000 Cabernet Sauvignon 146

Peninsula Ridge Estates Winery 2000 Cabernet Sauvignon Reserve 146

Peninsula Ridge Estates Winery 2000 Chardonnay Reserve 45

Peninsula Ridge Estates Winery 2000 Merlot 167

Peninsula Ridge Estates Winery 2000 Merlot-Cabernet Reserve 155

Peninsula Ridge Estates Winery 2000 Syrah 198

Peninsula Ridge Estates Winery 2000 Vidal Icewine 212

Peninsula Ridge Estates Winery 2001 Inox Chardonnay 45

Peninsula Ridge Estates Winery 2001 Sauvignon Blanc 98

Pillitteri Estates Winery 1999 Merlot Reserve 167

Pillitteri Estates Winery 2000 Cabernet Franc 132

Pillitteri Estates Winery 2000 Cabernet/Merlot Rosé 125

Pillitteri Estates Winery 2000 Gewürztraminer Riesling 115

Pillitteri Estates Winery 2000 Pinot Grigio 78

Pillitteri Estates Winery 2000 Riesling Icewine 218

Pillitteri Estates Winery 2000 Vidal Semi-Dry 110

Pillitteri Estates Winery 2001 Unoaked Chardonnay 53

Pillitteri Estates Winery 2001 Vidal Icewine 210

Pillitteri Estates Winery Spumante Classico 119

Quails' Gate Estate Winery 2000 Chenin Blanc Limited Release 105

Quails' Gate Estate Winery 2000 Family Reserve Cabernet Sauvignon 144

Quails' Gate Estate Winery 2000 Limited Reserve Merlot 176

Quails' Gate Estate Winery 2000 Pinot Noir Limited Release 185

Quails' Gate Estate Winery 2000 Riesling Icewine 218

Quails' Gate Estate Winery 2001 Chasselas-Pinot Blanc 113

Quails' Gate Estate Winery 2001 Dry Riesling Limited Release 89

Quails' Gate Estate Winery 2001 Gewürztraminer Limited Release 61

Quails' Gate Estate Winery 2001 Select Late Harvest Riesling 229

Reif Estate Winery 1999 Chardonnay Reserve Estate 45

Reif Estate Winery 1999 Vidal Icewine 210

Reif Estate Winery 2000 Cabernet Sauvignon 147

Reif Estate Winery 2000 Gewürztraminer Semi-Dry 58

Reif Estate Winery 2000 Late Harvest Riesling 230

Reif Estate Winery 2000 Meritage Estate Bottled 158

Reif Estate Winery 2000 Merlot 173

Reif Estate Winery 2000 Pinot Noir 188

Reif Estate Winery 2000 Vidal Icewine 209

Reif Estate Winery 2001 Gewürztraminer 64

Reif Estate Winery 2001 Riesling Estate Bottled 93

Reif Estate Winery 2001 Trollinger X Riesling Estate 107

St. Hubertus Estate Winery 2000 Bacchus 110

St. Hubertus Estate Winery 2000 Oak Bay Vineyard Maréchal Foch 205

St. Hubertus Estate Winery 2001 Oak Bay Vineyard Gewürztraminer 62

St. Hubertus Estate Winery 2001 Summer Symphony 225

Sandhill 2000 Cabernet Franc 136

Sandhill 2000 Merlot 174

Sandhill 2001 Chardonnay Burrowing Owl Vineyard 46

Sandhill 2001 Sauvignon Blanc Burrowing Owl Vineyard 99

Southbrook Winery 1998 Chardonnay Triomphe Chardonnay 46

Southbrook Winery 1998 Riesling Lailey Vineyard 89

Southbrook Winery 1999 Cabernet-Merlot Triomphe 159

Southbrook Winery 1999 Cabernet Sauvignon Lailey Vineyard 144

Southbrook Winery 1999 Chardonnay Lailey Vineyard 46

Southbrook Winery 1999 Chardonnay Triomphe 37

Southbrook Winery 1999 Merlot Lailey Vineyard 164

Southbrook Winery 2000 Blush 125

Southbrook Winery 2000 Chardonnay Triomphe 37

Southbrook Winery 2000 Vidal Icewine 212

Stonechurch Vineyards 1998 Cabernet Franc 136

Stonechurch Vineyards 1998 Cabernet Sauvignon Reserve 149

Stonechurch Vineyards 1999 St. David's Bench Reserve Chardonnay 46

Stonechurch Vineyards 1999 Vidal Icewine 213

Stonechurch Vineyards 2000 Cabernet Sauvignon 149

Stonechurch Vineyards NV Rosé Megan 127

Stoney Ridge Cellars 1997 Cuesta Estates Cabernet Franc 137

Stoney Ridge Cellars 1999 Bench Cabernet Franc 136

Stoney Ridge Cellars 1999 Bench Merlot 177

Stoney Ridge Cellars 1999 Bench Pinot Noir 189

Stoney Ridge Cellars 1999 Riesling Bench 93

Stoney Ridge Cellars 1999 Riesling Reserve 85

Stoney Ridge Cellars 1999 Vidal Icewine 213

Stoney Ridge Cellars 2000 Cabernet Franc Fox Vineyard Reserve 136

Stoney Ridge Cellars 2000 Chardonnay Bench 47

Strewn Wines 1994 Riesling 93

Strewn Wines 1998 Cabernet Sauvignon Terroir Strewn Vineyard 147

Strewn Wines 1998 Chardonnay Terroir Strewn Vineyard 53

Strewn Wines 1998 Late Harvest Vidal 231

Strewn Wines 1998 Riesling Süssreserve 89

Strewn Wines 1998 Riesling Terroir Strewn Vineyard 85

Strewn Wines 1998 Three Terroir 159

Strewn Wines 1999 Cabernet Franc 132

Strewn Wines 1999 Cabernet Franc Terroir 137

Strewn Wines 1999 Chardonnay Terroir Strewn Vineyard 38

Strewn Wines 1999 Gewürztraminer 64

Strewn Wines 1999 Merlot 177

Strewn Wines 1999 Pinot Blanc 69

Strewn Wines 1999 Two Vines Riesling Gewürztraminer 114

Strewn Wines 2000 Cabernet Franc 137

Strewn Wines 2000 Cabernet Franc Terroir Strewn Vineyard 140

Strewn Wines 2000 Cabernet Sauvignon Terroir Strewn Vineyard 147

Strewn Wines 2000 Chardonnay French Oak Terroir 47

Strewn Wines 2000 Merlot Terroir 177

Strewn Wines 2000 Sauvignon Blanc 99

Sumac Ridge Estate Winery 1998 Black Sage Vineyard Cabernet Sauvignon 147

Sumac Ridge Estate Winery 1998 Merlot Black Sage Vineyard 168

Sumac Ridge Estate Winery 1998 Pinnacle 159

Sumac Ridge Estate Winery 1998 Steller's Jay Brut Méthode Classique 118

Sumac Ridge Estate Winery 1999 Cabernet/Merlot 161

Sumac Ridge Estate Winery 1999 Merlot 168

Sumac Ridge Estate Winery 1999 Pinot Noir 189

Sumac Ridge Estate Winery 2000 Chardonnay Private Reserve 47

Sumac Ridge Estate Winery 2000 Gewürztraminer Private Reserve 59

Sumac Ridge Estate Winery 2000 Meritage (White) 111

Sumac Ridge Estate Winery 2000 Okanagan Blush 125

Sumac Ridge Estate Winery 2000 Pinot Blanc 70

Sumac Ridge Estate Winery 2000 Pinot Blanc Icewine 220

Sumac Ridge Estate Winery 2000 Pinot Blanc Private Reserve 68

Sumac Ridge Estate Winery 2001 Chardonnay Unoaked 38

Sumac Ridge Estate Winery 2001 Sauvignon Blanc 100

Sumac Ridge Estate Winery 2001 Sauvignon Blanc Private Reserve 100

Thirteenth Street Wine Co. 1998 G.H. Funk Vineyards Premier Cuvée 116

Thirteenth Street Wine Co. 1999 Sandstone Riesling Special Select Late Harvest 226

Thirteenth Street Wine Co. 2000 G.H. Funk Vineyards Riesling 85

Thirteenth Street Wine Co. 2000 Sandstone Cabernet Franc 133

Thirteenth Street Wine Co. 2000 Sandstone Meritage 161

Thirteenth Street Wine Co. 2000 Sandstone Reserve Chardonnay 38

Thirty Bench Wines 1999 Benchmark Merlot Cabernet Sauvignon Cabernet Franc Reserve 161

Thirty Bench Wines 1999 Cabernet Franc Benchmark Reserve 131

Thirty Bench Wines 1999 Cabernet-Merlot Tradition 161

Thirty Bench Wines 1999 Chardonnay Reserve Steve Kocsis Vineyard 47

Thirty Bench Wines 1999 Chardonnay Tradition 53

Thirty Bench Wines 1999 Merlot Reserve 177

Thirty Bench Wines 1999 Riesling Dry 94

Thirty Bench Wines 1999 Riesling Icewine 215

Thirty Bench Wines 1999 Riesling Limited Yield Semi-Dry 94

Thirty Bench Wines 1999 Riesling Special Select Late Harvest Estate Bottled 227

Thirty Bench Wines 1999 Trillium Blush 127

Thirty Bench Wines 2000 Cabernet Franc Tradition 140

Thirty Bench Wines 2000 Mountainview Blush 127

Thirty Bench Wines 2000 Mountainview White 114

Thirty Bench Wines 2000 Riesling 93

Thirty Bench Wines 2000 Riesling Icewine 218

Thirty Bench Wines 2000 Riesling Special Select Late Harvest Estate Bottled 226

Thomas and Vaughan Vintners 1999 Cabernet Franc 138

Thomas and Vaughan Vintners 1999 Cabernet Sauvignon Estate Reserve 149

Thomas and Vaughan Vintners 1999 Meritage 161

Thomas and Vaughan Vintners 2000 Cabernet Franc 140

Thomas and Vaughan Vintners 2000 Late Harvest Vidal 230

Thomas and Vaughan Vintners 2000 Maréchal Foch 204

Thomas and Vaughan Vintners 2000 Merlot Estate Reserve 177

Thomas and Vaughan Vintners 2000 Vidal Icewine 214

Thomas and Vaughan Vintners 2001 Maréchal Foch 204

Thomas and Vaughan Vintners 2001 Off-Dry Riesling 94

Thomas and Vaughan Vintners 2001 Pinot Gris 80

Thomas and Vaughan Vintners 2001 Vidal Semi-Sweet 107

Thornhaven Estates 2000 Chardonnay 54

Thornhaven Estates 2000 Pinot Noir 186

Thornhaven Estates 2000 Sauvignon Blanc–Chardonnay 114

Thornhaven Estates 2001 Gewürztraminer 59

Three Guys 2000 Pinot Noir Butler's Grant Vineyard 186

Tinhorn Creek Vineyards 2000 Cabernet Franc 140

Tinhorn Creek Vineyards 2000 Merlot 178

Tinhorn Creek Vineyards 2000 Pinot Noir 186

Tinhorn Creek Vineyards 2001 Pinot Gris 80

Vineland Estates Winery 1998 Late Harvest Vidal 227

Vineland Estates Winery 1999 Frontier Vineyard Reserve Gewürztraminer 62

Vineland Estates Winery 1999 Meritage 153

Vineland Estates Winery 1999 Riesling Méthode Cuvé Close 118

Vineland Estates Winery 1999 Riesling Reserve 86

Vineland Estates Winery 2000 Cabernet-Merlot Reserve 160

Vineland Estates Winery 2000 Chardonnay 48

Vineland Estates Winery 2000 Dry Riesling 82

Vineland Estates Winery 2000 Gewürztraminer 62

Vineland Estates Winery 2000 Meritage 155

Vineland Estates Winery 2000 Pinot Blanc 68

Vineland Estates Winery 2000 Pinot Gris 74

Vineland Estates Winery 2000 Sauvignon Blanc 100

Vineland Estates Winery 2000 Semi-Dry Riesling 86

Wild Goose Vineyards 2000 Merlot 168

Wild Goose Vineyards 2000 Riesling 90

Wild Goose Vineyards 2001 Autumn Gold 112

Wild Goose Vineyards 2001 Gewürztraminer 59

Wild Goose Vineyards 2001 Pinot Blanc 68

Wild Goose Vineyards 2001 Pinot Gris 75

Wild Goose Vineyards 2001 Riesling Dry Reserve 94

Willow Heights 1999 Chardonnay Stefanik Vineyard Reserve 48

Willow Heights Winery 1999 Vidal Icewine 214

A special offer for buying this book

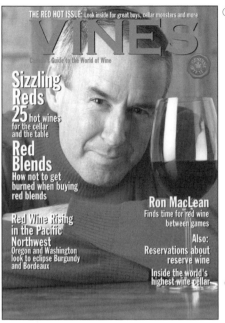

○ YES! Sign me up for a free trial subscription to Vines Magazine. This ballot entitles you to receive two free issues of Vines Magazine! If you like them, you can subscribe at our special rate of $19.95 for 12 issues (two years). That's **60% off the cover price**! If you don't choose to subscribe, simply write "cancel" on the subscription bill, and the free issues will be yours to keep. With no obligation.

name ....

address/apt ....

city/prov./p.code ....

○ From time to time, Vines Publishing allows clients to mail items which we believe to be of interest to our readers. If you wish to be excluded from such mailings please tick this circle

SIGN UP FOR A FREE TRIAL SUBSCRIPTION NOW!

A special offer for buying this book

○ YES! Sign me up for a free trial subscription to Vines Magazine. This ballot entitles you to receive two free issues of Vines Magazine! If you like them, you can subscribe at our special rate of $19.95 for 12 issues (two years). That's **60% off the cover price**! If you don't choose to subscribe, simply write "cancel" on the subscription bill, and the free issues will be yours to keep. With no obligation.

name ....

address/apt ....

city/prov./p.code ....

○ From time to time, Vines Publishing allows clients to mail items which we believe to be of interest to our readers. If you wish to be excluded from such mailings please tick this circle

SIGN UP FOR A FREE TRIAL SUBSCRIPTION NOW!

VINES Magazine
159 York St.
St. Catharines, ON
L2R 6E9

VINES Magazine
159 York St.
St. Catharines, ON
L2R 6E9